# ASK A LAWYER
## Wills and Trusts

ALSO BY STEVEN D. STRAUSS

The *Ask a Lawyer* series

Divorce and Child Custody

Landlord and Tenant

Debt and Bankruptcy

# ASK A LAWYER

# WILLS AND TRUSTS

Steven D. Strauss

W · W · NORTON & COMPANY

NEW YORK    LONDON

For information about permission to reproduce selections from this book, write to: Permissions, W. W. Norton & Company, Inc., 500 Fifth Avenue, New York, NY 10110.

The text of this book is composed in Berkeley Book, with the display set in Futura. Desktop composition by Chelsea Dippel. Manufacturing by the Haddon Craftsmen, Inc. Book design by Margaret Wagner.

Library of Congress Cataloging-in-Publication Data

Strauss, Steven D., 1958–
    Ask a lawyer. Wills and trusts / Steven D. Strauss.
       p.  cm.
    Includes index.
    **ISBN 0-393-04583-8. — ISBN 0-393-31728-5 (pbk.)**
    1. Wills—United States—Popular works. 2. Trusts and trustees—United States—Popular works. I. Title.
KF755.Z9S77 1998
346.7305'4—dc21                              97-33619
                                                      CIP

W. W. Norton & Company, Inc. 500 Fifth Avenue, New York, N.Y. 10110
http://www.wwnorton.com

W. W. Norton & Company Ltd., 10 Coptic Street, London WC1A 1PU

1 2 3 4 5 6 7 8 9 0

This book is dedicated to my beautiful children,
Jillian, Sydney, and Mara, whose estate I am trying to create.

Sincere thanks to Michael Pearce for his expertise and guidance in preparing this book.


Many thanks to Dori Stegman for everything she has done.

# CONTENTS

## III. WILLS

## IV. LIVING TRUSTS

## V. OTHER ESTATE-PLANNING OPTIONS

# VI. APPENDICES

# INTRODUCTION: ABOUT THIS BOOK AND THE *ASK A LAWYER* SERIES

A person usually needs an attorney either to act as an advocate or for advice. While there are many books on the market that endeavor to teach people how to be their own lawyer-advocate, this is not one of them. This book, and the *Ask a Lawyer* series, focuses upon the second function of an attorney—dispensing helpful, useful, and needed legal advice.

Few can afford to pay $250 to sit down with an attorney for an hour in order to get legal help. The *Ask a Lawyer* series is designed to give the advice of an attorney at a fraction of the cost. Helping people understand the law and their rights; explaining which of several options may work best for them; giving insights, tips, and helpful hints; in short, giving readers the type of assistance they would expect if they sat down with an expensive lawyer, *is* the purpose of this book and this series.

Deciding on an estate plan, in particular, is an area of the law that requires good legal help. As this book explains, there are a myriad of options available when someone begins to figure out how to leave his loved ones secure after his death. This book will help you figure out which options make the most sense. Should you have a will or a living trust? Just what is an "estate plan"? Do you need life insurance? Is probate really so bad? What kind of plan is right for you? Read on.

This book will sensibly walk you through the estate-planning process, caution you about possible pitfalls, explain in simple terms important aspects of the process, and guide you toward a plan that fits your needs. It is organized to make this often complicated area of the law quite easy to understand. Each chapter has its own table of contents, so that once you turn to a chapter of interest to you, you can quickly find the specific area with which you need help. If, for example, you have a question about naming guardians for your minor children in your will, flip to Chapter 13, titled "Choosing an Executor and a Guardian," and look under "Choosing a guardian."

Appendix A lists many common questions that often arise in the estate-planning process, along with sensible, simple answers. Any **boldfaced** word in this book can be found in the glossary, Appendix B.

No book of this type can come with a guarantee, and no book can substitute for the advice of an attorney familiar with your particular problems and issues. Nevertheless, this book can easily save you thousands of dollars in how your estate plan is handled. Absent many hours with high-priced legal counsel, this book is just about the next best thing.

# THE NEED FOR
# AN ESTATE PLAN

# LIFE AFTER DEATH

*Dying without a will or trust*

*Estate planning*

Howard and Suzanne had two small children, but after eight years of marriage, they separated. Howard's drinking had grown out of control, and Suzanne was worried that he was becoming a threat to their children. Because they were Catholic, they chose to separate instead of divorce. After Howard moved out, Suzanne and the children did not see him for more than two years; they did not know whether he was dead or alive.

On the way home from work one day, Suzanne died in a car accident. She had no will (she was "too young"). The probate court located Howard in a halfway house, and awarded guardianship of the children to him. They also gave Howard most of Suzanne's assets since he was still legally married to her.

DYING WITHOUT A WILL OR TRUST. When you die without a will or living trust, it is called dying **intestate.** Each state has a complex set of probate laws that determine how someone's property is to be distributed among his **heirs** should he die intestate. In most states, the surviving spouse gets half the **estate** (i.e., half of all property owned by the **decedent** at the time of death), and children divide the other half equally. If there are no children, then the surviving spouse often has to share the estate equally with the decedent's parents. If there is no living relative, the state will get everything owned by the decedent at the time of death.

Guardianship of any children is another matter altogether. A person who dies without a will forgoes the right to name the person who will raise his children. The state will decide this instead. Guardianship is usually awarded to the closest living relative.

Accordingly, the first of many benefits of having a **will** or **living trust** is that it guarantees that it is you, and not your state, who will decide what will happen to your property and children. Not many people want their state making such important decisions for them.

Yet most people avoid planning for life after death. Either it's too uncomfortable, or they think planning is a pain. Both reasons are faulty. Seen in the proper light, planning an estate should not be a burden. Almost every adult could benefit from some type of estate planning, even those who think estate planning is confined to the old and rich. In actuality, besides the old and rich, the people who probably need an estate plan include the middle-aged and well-off, as well as

- *Young adults:* No one knows when he will die. Even star athletes die in their prime. Drunk drivers, accidents, and health problems all account for thousands of deaths among young adults every year. Maybe you are right—maybe you will not die young. But what if you are wrong? Who will get your home? Who will care for your **minor** children? If you do not have at least a will, your state will decide these things for you.

- *Individuals without many assets:* Maybe you think that you do not have enough assets to warrant something that sounds as imposing as an **estate plan**. Wrong. Anyone who owns a home needs a will or living trust. And even if you do not own a home but you have certain property that you want a particular person to have, you need at least a will. Again, if you do not make some type of estate plan, your state has one for you as part of its probate laws.

· *People who think that they have handled it already:* Maybe you think that you don't need a will or living trust because you own property as **joint tenants** or because you live in a community property state. Owning property either way usually means that your spouse will automatically inherit everything. While true, this assumption is also misleading. Dying without a will or trust ensures that your property will go into **probate**. (See Chapter 7, "The High Cost of Dying: Probate.") In turn, probate ensures that much of your property will end up not with your family but in the hands of lawyers and your state in the form of probate fees and costs. A well-drafted estate plan can completely eliminate these costs, thereby putting more money in the hands of a mate or child.

If you want to avoid probate fees, if you want to avoid estate taxes legally, if one of your children needs help, if you want to name the guardian of your minor children, if you want your entire estate to be given to your spouse, if you want certain personal artifacts to go to a certain person, if you want a relative to get nothing, if you do not want your heirs to fight over who gets what, or if you want the bulk of your estate to go to your loved ones and not to probate lawyers and the IRS, then you need an estate plan.

ESTATE PLANNING. Although death may be an uncomfortable subject, planning how you want your assets divided and loved ones cared for when you die need not be. Properly done, creating an estate plan can be one of the most life-affirming things you will ever do.

In technical terms, an estate plan is any one of several legal methods available that create an orderly transfer of your property to your heirs upon your death. A good estate plan may also utilize a variety of estate-planning "tools" designed to accomplish your goals. These estate-planning tools include commonly thought of items such as wills and living trusts, but can also include things like **subtrusts**, jointly held property, **life insurance**, and **gifts**.

A good estate plan can also allow you to make medical decisions in advance if you ever become incapacitated by using a **durable health-care power of attorney** and a **living will**. (See Chapter 28, "Planning for a Disability.") It can pay taxes, buy homes, or care for children by using life insurance. (See Chapter 27, "Life Insurance.") Your estate plan can also do any of the following, depending upon the plan:

- *Reduce costs:* The legal process whereby assets are distributed to heirs is called probate. Probate is a time-consuming process that can end up costing the estate roughly 10 percent of its gross value in legal fees. Similarly, individuals with estates worth more than $600,000 must be concerned about estate taxes. A good estate plan can almost completely eliminate these costs. The money saved is money that ends up in the hands of your family.

- *Pick an executor or trustee:* In your will you pick the person who will wind up your affairs, called the **executor** of the estate (or, if it's a woman, the **executrix**). Similarly, your living trust is administered by your designated **trustee**.

- *Assist a charity:* A good estate plan can enable you to give money to a favorite cause, and receive corresponding tax benefits.

- *Keep your affairs private:* After you die, anyone who wants to can go to the probate court, obtain your file, and see what you left and to whom if you do not plan properly. A good estate plan can avoid this.

Notice the term "good estate plan"; not all estate plans are created equal. As a simple rule of thumb, living trusts are usually better than wills, and wills are better than nothing.

In real-life terms, an estate plan, then, is a way to make sure that your loved ones are taken care of in a manner you would want them to be after you die. It can care for children young and old, provide for a spouse, pay for college, buy a home, or pay for a wedding. It is a financial plan, a set of instructions, appropriate legal documents, and a plan of action all rolled into one.

By way of analogy, imagine that you and your spouse are about to take a long trip abroad without your children. What would you do before you go? You would think ahead and plan for any possible contingency. You would get someone you trust to care for your kids while you were gone. You would leave that person with enough money to take care of all necessities, and probably leave some extra in case of an emergency. You would likely leave a set of instructions as to how to care for each child, what each one likes and dislikes, and what each one may need. In essence, you would likely take all appropriate precautions and cover all bases. That is what an estate plan is.

*An estate plan is nothing more than a memo to those around you that explains how you want things handled when you are gone and gives your loved ones the resources to do those things.* Sure, it is couched in legal language. Yes, it sounds boring. But, properly done, an estate plan protects your assets and provides security for your loved ones. It is an affirmation of family and a commitment to your values. An estate plan is a life plan.

**The Important Legal Concept to Remember: Passing away without a will or living trust ensures that your priorities will not be taken into account when your state settles your affairs. A good estate plan is a plan that protects your family. It affirms your life's goals.**

**2**

# ON HIRING AND WORKING WITH A LAWYER

*Do you need a lawyer?*
*Finding a good attorney*
*Meeting with your attorney*

DO YOU NEED A LAWYER? The very first question to ask is whether a lawyer is even necessary to plan your estate. The answer is usually yes, but not always. It depends upon what you want to accomplish, and the size and complexity of your estate. If you want a simple will, you do not really need the assistance of an attorney. If you want a living trust, an attorney's help is a necessity.

How do you know if you need a will or a trust? As a *very* general rule, a will is sufficient if you are young and have little property. Wills are usually simple documents, and most attorneys can draft one for a couple of hundred dollars. The problem with a will is that it guarantees probate. Probate is a complex process, often taking a year or more, designed to accomplish the simple goal of transferring your property to your **beneficiaries**. Probate really should be avoided if at all possible. Nevertheless, if you are in your twenties or thirties, without a lot of property, then a basic will should suit your purposes just fine. You do not *have* to have a lawyer (although it is still usually a good idea).

Living trusts are different. Although a will can accomplish many estate-planning goals, a living trust is usually the better way to go. As explained in detail in Chapter 9, "Will or Trust?," in probably 90 percent of all cases in which someone is planning her estate, a living trust can accomplish the estate-planning goals better than a will, saving more money, ensuring total confidentiality, and totally avoiding probate. And if your estate is large (more than $600,000), a living trust is absolutely essential in order to avoid costly federal estate taxes. While drafting a simple will can probably be done without an attorney, creating a complex living trust cannot.

> Maria was an intelligent woman who owned her own business. Her first act of estate planning was to buy life insurance and name her daughter, Mara, as the beneficiary. Two years later, after the birth of her son, Mark, she decided to draft her own living trust. She bought a book that showed her how and went to work. She left everything she owned to Mara and Mark evenly.
>
> She did *almost* everything right, except that she forgot to change the beneficiary designation on her life insurance. When she died, her living trust made no difference because there was no money in it. Mara received the entire proceeds from Maria's life insurance and Mark got nothing.

FINDING A GOOD ATTORNEY. The very best place to find a good attorney is from a satisfied customer. Word-of-mouth advertising will tell far more about a lawyer than a dozen television commercials. If you know someone who has had her will or living trust done recently, find out how she liked her attorney, whether she was satisfied with the quality of the product, how long it took, whether the lawyer returned phone calls promptly, and how much money she spent.

Similarly, if you have a friend who is a lawyer, ask him, but do not hire him. There are more good lawyers than good friends around. Not only will you need to confess many intimate secrets to your attorney (who, by the way, has an obligation to keep them secret), but you may have to pay your friend a lot of money in the process. It is just far better to ask your lawyer friend's opinion about whom to hire than to hire him.

If you don't know any attorneys, and don't know anyone who knows any, then it gets a bit more difficult. Try to stay away from any referral services aside from that sponsored by your local **bar association**. Other referral services, found in the Yellow Pages, usually have but one requirement of the attorneys they recommend—money. Any lawyer who pays the fee required by the referral service will probably be recommended by that service. The local bar association is an organization of local lawyers, grouped by practice area, who often have a referral service based upon expertise, not profit.

Advisers are also a good source for finding an estate-planning attorney. Financial planners, accountants, life insurance agents, and bank trust officers are all in the estate-planning business in one form or another, and usually have extensive contacts with attorneys in the same field.

Prepaid group legal plans (provided through employment, unions, the American Association of Retired Persons, or the military) usually offer their members free wills as part of the plan. Living trusts usually cost something, but still less than the going rate for a private attorney. Low-cost legal clinics might provide adequate will planning, but should be avoided for living trusts.

The final option is advertising. Almost all attorneys, good and bad alike, now advertise. If a Yellow Page or television ad catches your fancy, and the lawyer practices in estate planning, schedule an interview and go speak with him.

MEETING WITH YOUR ATTORNEY. Expect to meet with your estate-planning attorney three times. The first meeting is basically an informational interview where you decide whether a

particular lawyer is right for you. This meeting should be free.
Most attorneys rarely charge when meeting with a new client
for the first time. Remember this: the attorney needs you more
than you need her, and competition among lawyers is fierce.
Check out a few different attorneys; it should cost you nothing,
and can make all the difference in how your case is handled.

Make sure to ask the following questions at this first meeting
with your potential lawyer:

- How long has she been in practice?
- Does she specialize in estate planning?
- Does she charge per hour, would she be willing to do the
  plan for a flat fee (that is, a set amount), and how much will
  it cost you?
- When will the work be done?
- Does she have any references (former clients) that you can
  speak with?

After you have found a lawyer whom you like, schedule the
second meeting. This is a nuts-and-bolts meeting where you
and your attorney design an estate plan, be it a will, trust, or
more. The more you organize the necessary information prior
to this meeting, the less your will or trust should cost. Most
attorneys charge by the hour, and even those who do not still
calculate their fees based, at least in part, on how much work
will be involved. The less she has to do, the better for your
pocketbook. A list of what you need to have ready should
include the following:

FAMILY

- Full names, addresses, occupations, and birth dates of you,
  your spouse, your children, and your grandchildren;
- Names and addresses of the chosen guardian(s) of your children;

- Your source of income, including employment, social security, disability, investment income, and all other sources of income;
- The date of your marriage, the date of dissolution for any previous divorces, and a list of all states you have lived in or plan to live in with your current spouse;
- Explanations of any disabilities, physical or mental incapacities, or special needs of any children or grandchildren;
- The names and addresses of any family members you specifically want to **disinherit**;
- All previous wills or living trusts.

MONEY

- A list of all checking and savings accounts, with account numbers;
- A list of all **real estate** that you own;
- A list of all financial investment accounts, with account numbers: stocks, bonds, CDs, annuities, mutual funds, money market accounts, treasury bills, IRAs and other retirement accounts, life insurance, disability insurance, profit-sharing plans, college funds, and limited partnerships. This list should indicate how title to the property is held. (See Chapter 5, "Taking Inventory.")
- An inventory of all **personal property**, such as furniture, cars, etc.

Bring your spouse to this meeting since there are many decisions that will have to be made about who will get what and the like. If your spouse is not there, the entire process will take more time and money.

Expect this meeting to take several hours. Not only will you need to go over all of this information with your attorney, decide who gets what, and figure out how any special needs of the family should be handled, but there are also many legal and tax factors that must be considered. The lawyer may recommend a simple will, a living trust, or a living trust with subtrusts. It depends on the unique circumstances of your family and financial situation.

After this meeting, your lawyer will get to work, and at your third meeting you will sign all wills, trusts, and other important legal documents. This entire process, from finding an attorney through the signing of the documents, should take about a month. You will not likely have any further contact with your estate-planning attorney unless you later decide to modify your plan.

**The Important Legal Concept to Remember: Not all attorneys are alike in personality or ability. Interview a few estate planning specialists and hire the one with whom you are most comfortable. After several meetings, expect to have a plan completed that is tailored specifically to your family.**

# WHAT YOU SHOULD EXPECT TO PAY

*Attorney fees*

*Keeping costs down*

ATTORNEY FEES. The cost of your estate plan depends almost entirely upon its complexity. A living trust, which attempts to avoid estate taxes, has special provisions for children, and contains health-care provisions, will obviously cost far more than a simple will.

A simple will, done without the assistance of lawyers, should cost almost nothing. A basic will drafted with the aid of an attorney should cost no more than a few hundred dollars. A paralegal can help with a will, but a word of caution is necessary: paralegals *are not* attorneys, and cannot give legal advice. All a paralegal can do is transcribe your decisions into the proper format.

More complicated estate plans utilize wills, living trusts, subtrusts, living wills, powers of attorney, and other estate-planning devices. The purpose of these plans is usually to avoid probate, taxes, or both. Prices can run anywhere from $500 to $10,000 or more, depending on the money involved, the complexity of the plan, and the number of options utilized.

Legal help is expensive. When you combine student loans, rent, payroll, malpractice insurance, ego, and greed, there is no way around it. Attorneys are paid to do things that laypeople usually cannot do themselves. Although you might be tempted to save money and draft a complicated estate plan yourself, don't.

Richard bought the most expensive computer program on the market and designed a living trust that he thought was foolproof. He bought life insurance. He drafted a living will. Although Richard's trust specifically stated that his home was to be part of the trust, he neglected to deed the house over to the trust. When he died, his home still went through probate.

The money saved by drafting a will or living trust yourself will be gobbled up in the first five hours of probate if you do it wrong.

KEEPING COSTS DOWN. Estate-planning attorneys can charge anywhere from $100 to $500 per hour based upon their locale and ability, although most will quote a flat fee for their services. Many living trust attorneys offer free seminars and oat fees. Because they have usually drafted thousands of living trusts, and everything is on computer, these plans are usually fairly inexpensive (e.g., under $1,000).

Even if you cannot get a flat fee, here are some tips that should help to decrease your legal fee:

- *Negotiate:* Everything is negotiable, even an attorney's bill. When meeting with an attorney for the first time, find out how much your will or trust will cost. When given an answer, try this negotiating technique: shake your head and do not say a word. The next word spoken, if you remain silent, should be your attorney reducing his estimate. Even if it is not, ask for a price 25 percent lower, and see where you end up. Remember, your attorney needs you more than you need him.

- *Get your attorney to agree not to charge for phone calls and other tasks that take less than five minutes:* If you are being charged by the hour, be sure to get your attorney to agree to not charge you for these simple tasks.

- *Get him to charge you his cost, and no more, for copies, faxes, etc.:* Law firms make a lot of money off the markup on administrative fees: twenty-five cents a page for a copy and one dollar a page for a fax are common. Copies should be about three cents, and faxes should be free.

- *Help him:* Any legwork that you do is time your attorney does not have to spend on your case. Organizing documents and making lists of assets can greatly help to reduce your fees.

**The Important Legal Concept to Remember: Good legal help is expensive. <u>Simple wills are less expensive than living trusts, and simple living trusts are less expensive than complicated living trusts.</u> No matter what estate-planning method you choose, remember that the first fee quoted by your attorney can almost always be reduced.**

# PLANNING YOUR ESTATE

# FORMULATING YOUR GOALS

*Formulating your goals*

*The five steps to planning an estate*

FORMULATING YOUR GOALS. Benjamin Franklin once re-
marked that you do not really know someone until you share
an inheritance with him. Whether the point of your estate plan
is to draft a will in order to name the **guardians** of your children and give away a few assets or to transfer to your adult children a million dollars, it should promote family unity. It should
not be something that divides a family, pitting brother against
brother, mother against daughter, yet the potential for that is
high. A properly funded estate plan, if not handled with care,
can bring out the greed in otherwise rational people.

Good estate planning is far more than the sterile act of merely giving your property away. It is, or at least it should be, a
process that analyzes your family situation and attempts to
address the hopes, needs, and desires of your family members.
When properly funded, a good estate plan is also a financial
tool that can ensure there is nothing to fight over. An estate
plan is a family plan and a financial plan, a safety net and a
dream launcher.

Because the possibility of misunderstanding and ill will do
run high, it may be useful to have a family meeting during the

planning stage, to gather ideas and create some type of consensus. This is especially true when adult children expecting to receive an **inheritance** are involved. If nothing else, this type of family meeting allows parents to explain why they may want to give different things, or disproportionate amounts of money, to different children.

The very first thing to do, then, when planning your estate is to size up the needs and desires of the family. What expenses will likely come due in the next twenty years? How much money will your spouse need to live on and to raise the children if you were to die today? What do your adult children need and expect? Do you just need to name a guardian for your minor children? Do you want to avoid estate taxes? Do you want your children to get their inheritance in one lump sum, or, maybe, at different times throughout their life? Does one child have special needs? Is there a charity you want to give some money to? Do you want to protect yourself in case of a disability? Do you want to avoid probate? It is the answers to questions like these that create the framework of your individual estate plan.

THE FIVE STEPS TO PLANNING AN ESTATE. The goal formulation just described is the first step in the estate-planning process. The second is to understand and inventory what you own in order to begin to decide how to accomplish your goals. The next chapter, "Taking Inventory," explains that process.

The third step is to decide who you want to get what you own. Chapter 6, "Who Gets What?," covers that process.

The fourth step is to analyze the financial impacts of any possible plan, including probate fees and taxes. Although there are few subjects less interesting than taxes in general, and estate taxes in particular, understanding the tax aspects of dying is often the *most critical* aspect to proper estate planning. (See Chapters 7 and 8, "The High Cost of Dying.")

The final and most complicated step is to decide on a plan utilizing the various estate-planning tools available. The plan should incorporate your goals, transfer what you own to whom you want, and protect every possible dollar in your estate. (See Chapter 9, "Will or Trust?")

**The Important Legal Concept to Remember:** Estate planning usually involves much more than writing a will. It is really a matter of assessing your life, your family, and your assets in order to create a later transfer of property that advances the lives of those you love.

# 5

# TAKING INVENTORY (YOU MAY NOT OWN AS MUCH AS YOU THINK YOU DO)

*The different ways to own property*

*Other property that cannot be given away in a will or living trust*

*Making an inventory*

You cannot give away, neither in will nor trust, that which you do not own. While seemingly obvious, it may surprise you to learn that you may not own nearly as much as you think you do. It all depends on how **title** to your property is held. Title is the legal definition of how property is owned. Title determines how much of a piece of property you *actually* own, as opposed to how much you *think you own*. Since you cannot give away in a will or trust that which you do not own, there can be no proper estate planning without first knowing how title to your property is held, and, therefore, how much property you actually have to give away.

Title is essentially synonymous with ownership. Title to property is not necessarily found on a piece of paper. Sometimes it is, sometimes it's not. The idea of title—how property is actually held—is usually thought of in regards to a deed to real estate. But the fact is, title applies to *all* property that you own, whether there is a title paper that goes with the property or not. Again, how you actually own your property, that is, how title is held, determines what you can give away.

*This cannot be emphasized enough.* If you attempt in your will or living trust to leave property to someone, and it later turns out that title was held in a manner that forbade such gifts (see below), then it is as if *no gift was ever made*; the trustee of your trust or the executor of your estate will have no choice but to ignore your **bequest**.

THE DIFFERENT WAYS TO OWN PROPERTY. How your property is owned governs what you can give away in your choice of estate plans. There are six ways to own property: sole ownership; tenancy in common; joint tenancy; and three forms of marital property ownership—tenancy by the entirety, community property, and joint marital assets.

1. **Sole ownership:** Sole ownership is when you own property outright, alone, without sharing it with a spouse or other co-owner. It is property that you bought with your own money and is used by you alone.

If you are single, almost everything you own is probably your sole property. Even if you still owe money on a car or home, it is still considered a sole asset for estate-planning purposes.

Can you have separately owned sole property if you are married? Yes, although it depends upon the property laws of your state. There are two state law systems for determining how title to property owned by married couples is held—**community property states** and **common law states**. Whether an asset is a sole possession depends upon which kind of state you live in. The nine community property states are Arizona, California, Idaho, Louisiana, Nevada, New Mexico, Texas, Washington, and Wisconsin. Puerto Rico is also a community property "state." All other states and the District of Columbia are common law states.

In *common law states*, all property owned prior to marriage, received as a gift or inheritance, or which is in one spouse's name alone is a sole separate asset of that spouse. If only one spouse's name appears on the title to a car, the car is a sole asset of that spouse. A gift made to a married person alone in one of these states—not to the couple—is also considered a separate asset.

Property bought with separate funds in a common law state is also solely owned by the purchaser. If you have a separate checking account that you used to buy a set of golf clubs, those clubs are your sole property.

Property bought with joint funds is joint property. If the clubs were bought with money from a joint account, they are not your separate property. They are a marital asset. Now, this does not mean that you and your spouse may not have an understanding that the clubs are really yours, and that you can give them away in a will to whomever you choose. You probably do. But what if the asset is a $5,000 bracelet bought from a joint account? Your spouse may object to you giving that away. It is for that reason that estate planning is best done together, so that there are no misunderstandings.

In a *community property state*, there are five categories of property that are considered separate:

1. Property owned prior to marriage;

2. Property bought while married using funds that can be traced to ownership prior to marriage;

3. Property acquired by either spouse during marriage through either gift or inheritance;

4. Property owned by the community that is intentionally, and in writing, given to the other spouse as his sole, separate property;

5. Property acquired after separation.

*Anything you own as a sole possession can be given away in your will or living trust as you wish.*

2. **Tenancy in common**: Tenancy in common is a way to own real estate among two or more persons. The distinguishing characteristic of a tenancy in common is that the property is shared proportionately by each person on the title, and each has an equal right to use the property. Ownership shares can be equal or unequal, depending upon the money invested and the agreement between the parties. A tenant in common can do whatever he wants with his *individual share*.

Larry, Jeff, and Jake bought an apartment house together as an investment, and decided to hold title as tenants in common. Each owns 33 percent of the entire building, and each is free to do whatever he wants with his share—give it away, sell it, or leave it to someone in a will.

If you own real estate, look at the deed. You will know whether you are able to **devise** (give away in a will) your share if the deed states that title is held as tenants in common. If it says "joint tenants," you cannot will your share away (see below.)

*If you own property as a tenant in common, you are free to give away your share, and your share only, in a will or living trust.*

3. **Joint tenancy**: As opposed to tenancy in common, whereby each person owns a divisible and proportional share of the property, joint tenancy means that both persons on the title own the *entire* property. Joint tenancy applies to real property and, less often, to bank accounts and other property. It is most often used by married persons who buy real estate together.

Joint tenancy is also sometimes called "joint tenancy with right of survivorship." That last clause is important, and is what distinguishes this type of property ownership. When one joint tenant dies, her share of the property *automatically* becomes the property of the other person named on the title. That is what "right of survivorship" means.

After they bought the apartment, Larry, Jeff, and Jake changed their minds and decided to hold title as joint tenants. When Jake passed away, his wife, Mindy, was shocked to learn that she owned *none* of the apartment. Because it was owned by joint tenants, Jake's share was *automatically* transferred to Larry and Jeff upon Jake's death.

The "right of survivorship" is a double-edged sword. As seen in the above example, unforeseen consequences can occur when property is held in joint tenancy. Yet, because the property does automatically become the property of the other joint tenant, *in very limited circumstances,* joint tenancy can be a fine estate-planning method. Because the property is transferred automatically at death, and since the point of probate is to transfer property, joint tenancy can be used to avoid probate. (Joint tenancy is fraught with potential problems. If it is of interest to you, make sure to read Chapter 25, "Joint Tenancy.")

If a husband and wife have a bank account held as joint tenants, then upon the death of either spouse, the entire amount in the account becomes the property of the other spouse.

*While the first joint tenant may attempt to give his share of the property away in a will or living trust, he legally cannot do so since his share is automatically transferred to the surviving joint tenant at death. Because neither joint tenant owns the property alone, joint tenancy property can be given away only after the death of the second, surviving, joint tenant. After the second joint tenant dies, the property will go to whomever is named in that person's will or living trust.*

4. **Tenancy by the entirety**: This form of real estate ownership is almost exactly like joint tenancy; that is, both parties own the whole property together, and if one dies, his share automatically goes to the other. The only difference is that tenancy by the entirety can be used only by married couples. Again, you must check the deed to your real estate to see how

your property is owned. Only about half the states allow tenancy by the entirety.

*If you own property as a tenancy by the entirety, you cannot give that property away in a will or trust because it is not yours alone to give away.*

5. **Community property**: As a reminder, the ten community property jurisdictions are Arizona, California, Idaho, Louisiana, Nevada, New Mexico, Texas, Washington, Wisconsin, and Puerto Rico.

In a community property state, you can devise only that property which is your sole, separate property and 50 percent of all property bought during marriage. In a community property state, generally speaking, all assets acquired by either spouse during marriage are considered jointly owned community property and belong jointly to *both* spouses. This includes all property bought by either spouse using any money earned while married, property bought with joint credit card or checking accounts, property bought with credit cards or checks in one person's name alone, and gifts made to the couple. It also includes property that is commingled, i.e., property that may at one time have been separate, but, because it was mixed in with community assets or money, is considered a community asset (separate money put in a joint bank account, for example). *Almost everything bought while married in a community property state becomes jointly owned community property.*

> Christopher had a lucrative job as a doctor. After they were married, he and Gretchen bought a house using both their credits. Christopher contributed 90 percent of the down payment, and Gretchen put in 10 percent. Gretchen owns 50 percent of the house.

You can tell whether an asset is separate or community by looking at the time of acquisition: if acquired during marriage, it is presumed community; if not, then it is not.

*In a community property state, you can give away to whomever you want all of your separate property and half of your community property.*

6. **Joint marital assets**: In the forty-one other common law states, ownership of joint marital assets is determined by *whose name is on the title*. If you own a home and your name appears on the title along with your spouse's, then you both own it, and it is a joint marital asset. If only your name is on the title, then it is your sole, separate property.

Joint marital assets, then, are those assets to which both names appear on the title (a deed, a bank account, a car), or for whose purchase joint income was used. If a husband and wife have separate bank accounts, and the wife uses her separate account to buy a car, the car is hers alone. It is important to note, though, that title trumps the source of money in these states. For example, if title to that car bought by the wife was put in both names, both spouses would own the car, despite the separate source purchase.

The ability to transfer marital property in a will or living trust really depends upon the laws of each common law state. As a general, but by no means steadfast, rule, *one must leave one's spouse at least 50 percent of all marital assets.* It is illegal to disinherit a spouse in every state. In community property states, disinheritance is impossible because each spouse already owns 50 percent of any item. In common law states, it is usually illegal not to give a spouse 50 percent.

*In the forty-one common law states and the District of Columbia, you can give away your sole, separate property and half of your marital property however you wish, in either a trust or a will. The other half of all marital property must normally be given to your spouse.*

OTHER PROPERTY THAT CANNOT BE GIVEN AWAY IN A WILL OR LIVING TRUST. Besides the property listed above, some of which cannot be given away after death, there are a few other types of assets that also cannot be given away in a will or trust.

The most common type is that property which requires a beneficiary designation. A good example is life insurance. A life insurance policy names a beneficiary. No will or living trust can change that. Whoever is the named beneficiary will get the property, despite what any will says. Similar beneficiary-designated property includes retirement benefits and certain kinds of bank accounts.

MAKING AN INVENTORY. With the above information, it is now possible to make a list of all assets that you actually own. This list will be invaluable to your attorney, saving you a lot of money.

**The Important Legal Concept to Remember: You cannot give away that which you do not own, thus you must have a thorough understanding of the actual contents of your estate before you can formulate any estate plan. In common law states, property ownership is largely dependent upon how title is held. In community property states, ownership usually depends upon when the property was acquired.**

# 6

# WHO GETS WHAT? (NAMING YOUR BENEFICIARIES)

*Classifications of beneficiaries*
*Having beneficiaries share property*
*Leaving property to a pet*
*Leaving instructions*

It may seem obvious to you who will be inheriting the property you own. Nevertheless, there are some rules for giving gifts after death that you must know about to guarantee that what you own does in fact go to whom you want.

CLASSIFICATIONS OF BENEFICIARIES. A **beneficiary** is the person, charity, or organization to whom you will leave money or property. There are four types of beneficiaries: primary, alternate, residuary, and alternate residuary. Each person or entity that is to receive your property falls into one of these four categories.

1. **Primary beneficiaries**: As the name indicates, a primary beneficiary is the main person who will receive a piece of your property. Each person who is to receive property or money is a primary beneficiary.

Gayle wants her home to go to her daughter Emma, and her money to go to her son Sidney. Emma and Sidney are Gayle's primary beneficiaries.

2. **Alternate beneficiaries**: Should one of your primary beneficiaries die before you do, it is a good idea to name someone else to get the property that person would have received. If a primary beneficiary is young, then there may be no need to name an alternate since the likelihood of her dying before you is remote. If a primary beneficiary is older, then naming an alternate is smart. Alternate and primary beneficiaries go hand in hand—it is good planning to name them together for any single piece of property.

Gayle named Emma's husband as the alternate beneficiary for her house if Emma should die first. If her son Sidney should predecease her, Gayle named the American Cancer Society as the alternate beneficiary for her money.

3. **Residuary beneficiary**: A residuary beneficiary is a different animal altogether. It is highly unlikely that you will specifically give away each particular piece of property that you own to a specific primary beneficiary. Far more likely is a will or living trust that will state something such as: "Anything not specifically given away is given to my husband." The husband is the residuary beneficiary, and all those other "things" are the **residuary** of the decedent's estate. The residuary often encompasses the bulk of someone's estate. Because of this, it is often the most important clause in a will or living trust.

Besides her house and money, Gayle had a lifetime's worth of furniture, some investments, and a beloved dog. Gayle named her brother Stuart to be the beneficiary of the residuary of her estate.

4. **Alternate residuary beneficiary**: Just as a primary and alternate beneficiary go together, so too do a residuary and alternate residuary beneficiary.

Gayle named her children as the alternate residuary beneficiaries of her estate should Stuart die first.

The essence of all of these designations is that you must
think through carefully whom you want to get your things, and
what you want to happen if someone you name as a beneficiary dies before you. You then relate this in your will or trust.

HAVING BENEFICIARIES SHARE PROPERTY. A common desire for
many people is to have more than one person share a large
gift. Several problems are possible if care is not taken.

After thinking things through, Gayle decided that it would
be more fair if Emma and Sidney shared her house, so she
left it to them jointly. After Gayle passed away, Sidney wanted to live in the house but Emma wanted to sell it. After
many fights, the siblings stopped talking to each other.

The issue, then, of who will manage the asset is an important
consideration. It may be best to name one heir as the final decision maker regarding the property, although this could create
a different set of problems. Similar issues arise with regard to
percentages of ownership—will the property be owned equally or in different percentages? If you want your children to
own your house in different proportions (maybe because one
child is better off financially than the other), then the percentage shares must be specified in the will or trust. This too can
certainly become a source of friction.

There are three solutions to this dilemma:

1. As indicated previously, a family meeting can resolve many of
   these issues before they ever arise.
2. Have the will or trust state that the particular piece of property is to be sold and that the *proceeds* are to be divided
   equally or unequally—however you wish.
3. Simply do not leave a shared gift.

LEAVING PROPERTY TO A PET. Only Tennessee and California allow people to leave money or property to a pet. If you try to do so in the forty-eight other states or in the District of Columbia, the court will ignore this bequest. It will take the property given to the pet, add it to your residuary estate, and give it to your residuary beneficiary. What you can do instead if this is your desire is to leave your pet, and some money for care of that pet, to someone who you know will care for the animal.

LEAVING INSTRUCTIONS. It is generally a good idea to leave some lasting thoughts with your will or trust explaining why you did what you did, if your beneficiaries do not already know. These thoughts/instructions can be part of the estate document, or can be in the form of a letter accompanying the document. If a letter is left, it is important that it expressly states that it is not a **codicil** to the will (a modification) or a change in the terms of the trust.

**The Important Legal Concept to Remember: Good estate planning requires deciding which beneficiaries get what property, and what should happen if they do not outlive you. Leaving lasting thoughts is usually appreciated. Leaving a shared gift often is not.**

# 7

# THE HIGH COST OF DYING: PROBATE

*What probate is*

*The probate process*

*Probate fees and costs*

*How to reduce or even completely avoid probate fees*

WHAT PROBATE IS. One of the important things to consider when analyzing estate-planning options is the possibility of probate. When a person passes away, he leaves property behind. Probate is the process that courts use to determine the validity of a will, make sure that all creditors get paid, and transfer that property to the decedent's heirs.

Probate occurs when the deceased either dies with a valid will (called dying testate) or dies without a will at all (called dying intestate.) The only time probate is not needed is if the decedent used a living trust or some other probate-avoiding estate-planning methods, such as **pay-on-death accounts** and others. (See Section V, "Other Estate-Planning Options.")

Avoiding probate is often a main estate-planning goal, and it should be. Probate is a very lengthy, expensive process. It is complicated. It is difficult for bereaved family members. It should be avoided if at all possible. And, it is possible.

THE PROBATE PROCESS. There are several steps to probating an estate. First, a probate case must be opened. The executor named in the will must locate the original will and submit it to the probate court. If there is no will, then a relative or creditor (called an **interested person**) must file a written request to open up a probate proceeding. The first thing that will occur in that case is that an administrator or **personal representative** will be appointed to act in the same capacity as an executor. He or she will oversee the process and shepherd the transfer of property through the courts.

After the executor is named, heirs are ascertained, beneficiaries are notified, all property is located and valued, creditors are informed of the proceedings, legitimate creditor claims are paid, taxes are filed and paid, and a final accounting of debts, costs, and property valuations is made. If an heir is unhappy with the will, she may initiate a **will contest** in an attempt to modify or completely disregard the will. (See Chapter 14, "Will Contests.") Only after all taxes and creditor claims have been ascertained and paid, and after all attorney fees, court costs, and executor fees are paid, is the remaining money and property (if any) finally distributed among the heirs of the deceased.

It is not uncommon for probate to last *two years*. The only time probate may be quick is when the gross value of the estate is small—$50,000 or less, for example, depending on the state. In those cases, each state has an expedited probate process that takes a few months.

PROBATE FEES AND COSTS. Probate fees and costs can be broken down into three categories.

The first are the fees paid to the executor. The job of executor or personal representative is demanding. He or she spends many hours sorting through the affairs of the deceased, time that is compensated out of the assets of the estate. Another cost borne by the executor are appraisal fees, which are incurred to determine the value of the estate. Since attorney fees and executor fees are sometimes paid as a percentage of the *gross value of the estate*, an accurate appraisal of the estate is often needed.

The second expense is court costs. This includes things like filing fees, costs associated with publication of notices in newspapers, and docket fees. These fees usually run around $1,000.

By far, the costliest part of probate is the fees spent on lawyers. Attorney fees usually run between 3 and 20 percent of the gross value of the estate, and can run much higher if "extraordinary" services are rendered. Extraordinary services consist of things like litigation within the probate or transference of real property.

Again, it is very important to understand that the value of an estate is based on its *gross value*; that is, the value of all property (i.e., the "estate") *before* subtracting anything for debts. Just as a $200,000 home with a $100,000 mortgage is still worth $200,000, so too is an estate that is worth $200,000 with $100,000 in debts still worth $200,000. And it is that gross value—that $200,000—which determines the value of an estate, and, therefore, how much probate will cost your heirs.

> Michael's $100,000 home was paid off. When he died, the cost of probate was 6 percent of the gross value of the estate—$6,000. Because the house was paid off, 6 percent reflected the true cost of probating the estate.
>
> Rosa's $100,000 home had a $90,000 mortgage left when she died. The cost of probate was also 6 percent of the gross value of her estate—$6,000. However, as a percentage of the *real* value of the estate, which was actually $10,000, the $6,000 consumed 60 percent of the estate.

Smaller estates pay a higher percentage in probate fees than larger estates. A typical breakdown goes something like this:

| GROSS VALUE | PROBATE FEES |
| --- | --- |
| $100,000 | $6,000 |
| $150,000 | $8,500 |
| $250,000 | $12,000 |
| $500,000 | $22,000 |
| $1,000,000 | $40,000 |

The important thing, then, when planning your estate, is to estimate objectively and accurately its gross value so that any potential probate fees can be determined, and, hopefully, avoided.

HOW TO REDUCE OR EVEN COMPLETELY AVOID PROBATE FEES. Probate has a deservedly bad reputation. It takes too long. It is too expensive. All the fees spent in probate is money that could and should be in the hands of your loved ones. And your estate need not pay these fees. Proper estate planning can reduce probate costs, even eliminate them entirely, and keep your money with those you love. There are ways to transfer your property so that probate can be avoided. The most common methods are living trusts, life insurance, gifts, joint tenancy, and pay-on-death accounts. (See Section IV, "Living Trusts," and Section V, "Other Estate-Planning Options.")

**The Important Legal Concept to Remember: Probate is a clumsy, time-consuming, expensive maze of a process and should be avoided in most cases.**

# 8

# THE HIGH COST OF DYING: TAXES

*Federal estate taxes on estates over $600,000*
*State death and inheritance taxes*
*Other possible taxes*
*Estate planning tax tips*

Aside from costly probate fees, another major consideration when planning an estate is the possibility of estate taxes. Understand that probate fees and estate taxes are two different types of possible costs to one's estate. The methods used to avoid probate fees are different from those used to avoid estate taxes. Estate taxes are not avoided simply because probate is.

FEDERAL ESTATE TAXES ON ESTATES OVER $600,000.* *State* estate taxes, discussed below, are a relatively minor issue in estate planning as they do not usually constitute a large tax burden. *Federal* estate taxes are another matter. The potential federal tax liability on a large estate is a major concern, and sometimes *the* major concern, when planning an estate.

Federal estate taxes, while a very complicated area of the law, can be reduced to six simple rules. Understand these rules, and the rest is easy.

*Rule 1. Federal estate taxes apply only to the net value of your*

*According to recent legislation, this figure will escalate to $1 million by 2007.

*estate:* Recall that probate fees are calculated as a percentage of the gross value of an estate. This is not so for estate taxes. Federal estate taxes are based upon the **net value** (assets less liabilities) of an estate. This is called your **taxable estate**.

*Rule 2. Federal estate taxes apply only when the taxable estate exceeds $600,000 per individual:* If the taxable estate is less than $600,000, there will be *no* federal **death taxes**. When the value of an individual estate exceeds $600,000, estate taxes kick in at 37 percent.

Although you may think that your estate is not worth $600,000, keep in mind that everything you own goes into the calculation: real estate, investments, cars, life insurance policies, businesses, farms, and retirement, pension, and profit-sharing plans. Life insurance in particular must not be overlooked.

It is also important to realize that your estate's net value today is probably less than what it will be when you die.

Don's estate was worth $500,000 before he died. He also had a $250,000 life insurance policy naming his son as the sole beneficiary. Don's taxable estate is worth $750,000.

Another possible problem is that although your estate may not be worth $600,000, your spouse's taxable estate may exceed that amount after she receives her inheritance from you.

John's estate was worth $350,000 and he inherited his wife, Julie's, entire estate, also worth $350,000. Because John inherited Julie's entire estate, when he died, his estate was worth $700,000. The $100,000 over the $600,000 ceiling was taxed at 37 percent.

*Rule 3. Anyone can leave anyone else up to $600,000 tax-free:* Because no tax is due on any estate worth less than $600,000, it follows that anyone can leave anyone else up to that amount without having to pay federal estate taxes. This is called the unified tax credit.

> Eric had an estate worth $600,000. When he died, each of his two children received $300,000. No tax was due.

*Rule 4. A spouse can give his mate any amount, tax-free:* Married partners can leave their entire estate, no matter the size, to their mate and no tax will be owed. If Phil and Mindy are worth $4 million, Phil can leave Mindy his $2 million and she will owe *no tax* on that money. This is called the unlimited marital deduction. This unlimited marital deduction is *above and beyond* the $600,000 unified tax credit.

> Gina has an estate worth $2.6 million. At her death, Gina can leave $600,000 to her children, and $2 million to her husband, Dennis. The children will not pay taxes on their amount due to the $600,000 unified credit, and Dennis will not pay taxes on his $2 million due to the unlimited marital deduction.

The potential problem with this is that when the surviving mate dies, his estate *will* owe taxes on the *entire amount* remaining. In the case of Dennis and Gina, Dennis's estate will owe death taxes not only on his own $2 million but on the $2 million he inherited from Gina as well. The unlimited marital deduction, then, really only postpones the inevitable tax bite from Uncle Sam. In order to avoid this result, a special subtrust of a living trust can be set up that enables partners to transfer $1.2 million to their children tax-free. (See Chapter 19, "Trusts for Spouses.")

*Rule 5. You can give up to $10,000 yearly to anyone tax-free:* IRS regulations let any taxpayer give away up to $10,000 (or any married couple, up to $20,000) yearly, per recipient, without paying any gift or inheritance tax. This is called the annual exclusion.

Alan had an estate worth $700,000. Knowing this, he gave each of his two sons $10,000 a year for five years ($100,000 total). Upon his death, his two sons split the remaining $600,000, and no death tax was owed.

*Rule 6. All gifts made to charity are tax-free:* Any gift of any amount made to a tax-exempt charity during your life or upon your death is free from any federal estate or gift tax.

That's it. These six rules form the basis of 99 percent of all living trust plans. When an estate is worth more than $600,000, estate planning consists of utilizing various methods, most notably living trusts, in order to take advantage of these six rules.

One final note: Congress can change federal estate tax laws at any time. While the $600,000 figure consistently mentioned herein reflects the current state of the law, that figure is not set in stone. This is just one more reason why living trusts are best accomplished when working in unison with an estate planning attorney.

STATE DEATH AND INHERITANCE TAXES. State death and inheritance taxes are applicable to some degree in every state except Nevada. Some states tax only those estates larger than $600,000, as the federal government does. Other states tax only real estate owned in the state, while others tax personal property. Usually, however, the amount taxed is not significant.

By checking with an attorney in your area, you can learn whether your state is one of the ones that impose significant state death taxes. If so, one method to lower your estate's potential tax liability is to change your **domicile**. Your domicile is where you primarily live. You can have only one domicile. If you have connections with more than one state, it might be possible to name the state with the lower state death taxes as your domicile. For example, if you live in one state but have a vacation home in another, you might name the other state as your domicile without ever moving. You can thereby save taxes and preserve your estate for your family.

OTHER POSSIBLE TAXES. Aside from federal and state death taxes, there are three other possible taxes that may be applicable to your estate.

First are possible taxes on tax-deferred employee compensation plans (pension plans, retirement plans, Keoghs, etc.). Such plans usually have named beneficiaries, and death benefits under these plans usually pass to the beneficiary tax-free. If, however, the proceeds are payable to your estate, then the amount received becomes part of your taxable estate. To the extent that this may raise your estate above the magical $600,000 figure, designating your estate as the beneficiary of your policy may be unwise (unless some of the tax-saving tips outlined below are utilized).

The second possible tax is a **capital gains tax**. When you own assets that grow in value appreciably, a tax must be paid on the profit—a capital gains tax. Because there are so many costs associated with dying, such as attorney fees, court costs, and administrative fees, a large piece of the estate is often sold in order to pay these costs. If the property has been owned for some time, then the potential capital gains tax could be significant.

The final tax you should know about is a tax on the proceeds of life insurance if the proceeds are paid to an estate, trust, or trustee. Insurance benefits payable to individuals are not taxed to the individual. If you want to name your trust as a beneficiary (so that your trustee can oversee the use of these often large sums) and still avoid possible taxes, then you need to have an irrevocable life insurance trust (an **ILIT**) created. (See Chapter 21, "Other Types of Subtrusts.")

ESTATE-PLANNING TAX TIPS. If your estate's value is at least $600,000, or if your spouse's will exceed that amount when you leave your estate to her, then there are at least three methods to reduce this potential tax bite:

1. *Use a trust:* There are several tax-savings trusts that you can set up, discussed in detail in Section IV, which reduce or eliminate taxes.

2. *Give a gift:* As indicated, any one person can give up to $10,000 a year away per recipient tax-free. A married couple can give away $20,000 a year tax-free per recipient. (See Chapter 24, "Gifts.")

3. *Transfer your life insurance:* Life insurance is an important element to most estate plans. For a relatively small amount of money, the policy ensures that one's family will be financially stable. The downside of life insurance is that should the proceeds become part of the taxable estate, the $600,000 tax-exempt ceiling can be reached very quickly. Chapter 27, "Life Insurance," explains two different ways to avoid estate taxes on life insurance proceeds.

**The Important Legal Concept to Remember: Taxes are often a difficult subject to know well. Nevertheless, tax considerations are among the most important, and often *the* most important, aspects of estate planning. Knowing the six rules of taxes can save your family hundreds of thousands of dollars.**

# 9

# WILL OR TRUST?

*Advantages to using a will*
*Disadvantages to using a will*
*How to use a will and still avoid probate*
*Living trusts*
*Advantages to using a trust*
*Disadvantages of a living trust*
*Which one is best for you?*

An estate plan can be as simple as a one-page will or as complicated as a living trust with several subtrusts incorporating an insurance package, a living will, powers of attorney, and charitable gifts. Either way, the main question is whether a will or a living trust makes more sense as the basic estate-planning device.

ADVANTAGES TO USING A WILL. Wills have been around since before biblical times. They are a time-tested method of transferring property you own to people you love after you die.

The advantage of having a will is self-evident. You get to choose what happens to your property and children after you are gone, thereby taking these critical decisions out of the hands of your state legislature. Wills also have the added advantage of being **revocable**—you can change your will at any time, add to it, subtract from it, even revoke it totally in favor of a new will or a living trust. Another real advantage of a will is that it is usually a far simpler document than a living trust, and is accordingly much more affordable.

Wills are also the only document that one can use to name guardians for minor children. If you are a parent of small children and are planning to use a living trust, you will still need a basic will.

DISADVANTAGES TO USING A WILL. Far and away the most negative aspect of a will is that it ensures probate, and probate is an expensive, time-consuming drain on resources and emotions. Especially since probate is fairly easily avoided, wills and probate often make little sense.

Other problems with choosing a will as a primary estate-planning device are

- *Wills are public:* Wills are public documents since probate is a public court proceeding. Anyone who wants to can go down to the courthouse and see how much you left and to whom you left it.
- *Wills apply only at death:* A will is a document that attains legal importance upon your death. Prior to that, its legal effect is zero.
- *A lot can go wrong:* If a will is improperly drafted, signed, or witnessed (called **execution**), the will is useless. Moreover, if the will maker moves out of state after getting a perfectly executed will, the will may be inapplicable in the new state. The intended outcome of the will may also change due to different laws in the new state. Even worse, unhappy heirs can attack a perfectly good will in probate court fairly easily.

Almost all of these problems can be avoided with a living trust.

HOW TO USE A WILL AND STILL AVOID PROBATE. Many people still prefer to use a will instead of a living trust, especially in light of the cost difference, regardless of any flaws. If this applies to you, know that it is still possible to avoid probate.

The first method depends upon how your property is held. Recall that certain property, most notably joint tenancy property, transfers automatically to a named beneficiary at the death of the other co-owner. One simple and inexpensive way to plan your estate, then, especially if you are young or otherwise without significant assets, is to have a will drawn up, and to use some of the will substitutes found in Section V. By so doing, and by holding title to any significant assets as joint tenants, you ensure that your property will go to whom you want, and that probate will be avoided.

The second way that a will can be used and probate still avoided is when the gross value of the estate is relatively small. Probate laws differ in each state, but each does have a small-estate exception allowing property in an estate under a certain dollar figure to be transferred outside probate. The size of the estate falling within the exception ranges from $5,000 to $60,000, depending on the state.

LIVING TRUSTS. There are basically two types of trusts: trusts made while you are alive, called, not coincidentally, living trusts; and trusts created as part of your will that apply only after your death, called **testamentary trusts.** (There are also many sorts of subtrusts of each type of trust, depending upon what you want to accomplish.)

Since one of the main reasons for deciding to use a trust is to avoid probate, a living trust is better than a testamentary trust. Because a testamentary trust is part of a will, your entire estate will still need to go through probate in order to fund the testamentary trust. It is a self-defeating document. Living trusts, on the other hand, become effective while you are alive, and therefore avoid probate.

Here is how living trusts work: After deciding all the particulars of your desired estate plan, you go to a lawyer who will draft your trust for you in accordance with your wishes. You name yourself as both trustee and beneficiary of the trust, and transfer all of your assets into the trust. Because you are the trustee as well as the beneficiary of your trust, you continue to use and own all of your property, just as you always have. However, because your living trust is a separate legal entity, and because you put all of your assets into this entity which you control, when you die there is nothing to probate. It is your trust and not you who owns all of your property.

ADVANTAGES TO USING A TRUST. Besides the obvious advantage of probate avoidance, a properly drafted and funded living trust has the following positive additional aspects:

- *Taxes:* Estates of $600,000 or more currently have a potential tax liability starting at 37 percent. For a married couple, an **A-B trust** or **bypass trust** (one type of living trust subtrust) helps to reduce or avoid this possibility.

- *Privacy:* Even if you do not have an estate that necessitates an A-B trust, that a living trust is a completely private document is often reason enough to select this estate-planning option.

- *Flexibility:* A living trust is also sometimes called a revocable living trust because it can be revoked, changed, or otherwise altered however you want, whenever you want. You can add assets, delete beneficiaries, or change trustees.

- *Disability:* One aspect of a living trust that appeals to older people is the ability to plan in case of a disability. Choosing a conservator prior to getting ill saves both the expense involved in court proceedings and the possibility that the court may choose the wrong person.

- *Control:* A living trust allows you to retain complete control over your property during your life. If you should become disabled, the trust also lets you, and not a court, control who will manage your affairs.

- *Speed:* Assets that go through probate are distributed to the heirs only at the very end of the probate process, often two years after the death. A living trust will allow your property to go to your beneficiaries far more quickly upon your death.

DISADVANTAGES OF A LIVING TRUST. Living trusts are not perfect:

- *Expense:* Living trusts are more expensive to set up than wills. For younger people the expense may not be worth the benefit.
- *Redundant:* Even if you have a living trust, you will still probably need a will for reasons previously stated.
- *Protection:* Because in most states creditors have a very limited amount of time to file claims against your estate in probate court (called the statute of limitations), they may have more time to come after your estate's assets if you have a living trust.
- *Challenges:* An unhappy heir can certainly attack a will easier than a living trust in the probate court, but this is not to say that she cannot challenge a living trust as well in civil court.

WHICH ONE IS BEST FOR YOU? It is easy to advise that the advantages of living trusts make them the preferable tool of basic estate planning for most people. It is true, albeit not entirely.

Although living trusts are a superior planning device in most cases, most cases are not all cases. A will makes sense if your main goal is to name a guardian for your minor children and/or transfer a few possessions. A will also works if you are young, without significant assets, and realistically will probably not die soon. If you don't want to spend a lot of money, get a will.

If you expect to be making or inheriting money later in life you might also consider using a will. Since a living trust needs assets to function, there is no need to create one if there are no assets to fund it. In that case, a will, when combined with life

insurance and other will substitutes, creates a perfectly acceptable estate plan. A living trust can always come later, when its
advantages can be utilized.

Conversely, if you are older or have a lot of assets, then a
living trust is almost certainly a better choice. The potential
tax savings alone are reason enough to get a living trust. When
combined with the ability to use and control your trust property during your life, help children, plan for a disability, avoid
probate, and keep your affairs private, the decision almost
becomes compelling.

**The Important Legal Concept to Remember: Choosing
between a will and a living trust is the single most important estate-planning decision you will make. Usually, a living trust makes a lot more sense than a will.**

# III

# WILLS

# 10

# WILLS MADE EASY

*Wills*
*Will formalities*
*Contents of a basic will*
*Types of wills*
*What a will cannot do*

WILLS. A will is a simple document with an important purpose. It is nothing more than a set of instructions that indicate what you want done with your property after you die. Because substantial amounts of money are usually involved when a will is probated, the law wants to make sure that a will admitted into probate is really the will of the deceased. It does so by making certain aspects of will making *mandatory*; as long as the will contains the necessary provisions and is executed in the proper fashion, the desires of the **testator** will be carried out.

WILL FORMALITIES. Each state has slightly different requirements for a will to be valid. If any of these formalities are missed, the will will be thrown out of court and the estate will be probated as if no estate planning occurred. The most common requirements are these:

• *The age requirement:* All states except Georgia require a person to be at least eighteen years old to make a will. In Wyoming the age is nineteen; in Georgia, fourteen.

- *The competency requirement:* In order to make a legally enforceable will, the testator must be of sound mind and memory. He must know what he is doing, understand the nature and extent of his property, and specifically intend to execute the will. The witnesses will then attest in the **affidavit** that the testator was of sound mind and knew what she was doing at the time of the signing.

- *The writing requirement:* Although a will in one's own handwriting is valid in certain limited circumstances, to ensure the validity of a will, have it typed or word-processed.

- *The signing requirement:* The will must be signed and dated by the testator in front of witnesses. It should contain a statement that it is her will and that she did in fact sign it in the presence of witnesses. The only time a lack of signing may possibly be excused is when illiteracy or illness prevents it. Properly signing and witnessing the document is called the execution of the will. *Proper execution is elemental to a valid will.*

- *The witness requirement:* Depending on the state, two or three witnesses are necessary to view the actual signing of the document by the maker of the will. To be safe, include three. Then, in front of the testator, the witnesses will sign the affidavit certifying that they witnessed the signing by the testator. The witnesses should be disinterested—they should not receive anything in the will. Witnessing too is part of the execution of the will. *Proper execution is elemental to a valid will.*

- *The substantive provision requirement:* The will must do something: it must either name a guardian for minor children or dispose of some property.

- *The executor provision:* The executor is the person who will carry out the terms of the will. Although not a necessity, it is a very good idea to name an executor.

CONTENTS OF A BASIC WILL. Incorporating these requirements into a will is a simple matter. A will is usually three pages or so in length, although complicated wills that give away a lot of money can be more than one hundred pages. Properly drafted wills should contain the following provisions:

- *A revocation clause:* The first clause in a will revokes all previous wills. Imagine the problems that would ensue if two different, equally valid wills were discovered in the testator's belongings and presented to the court. A sentence that states "I revoke all previous wills and codicils [modifications of a previous will]" avoids that possibility.

- *A family status clause:* The will should state your marital status and name your spouse. It should also name your children and give their dates of birth.

- *A payment of necessary expenses clause:* The will should authorize your executor to pay funeral expenses, last illness expenses, enforceable unsecured debts (not all debts are enforceable), and other necessary expenses.

- *A bequest clause:* The will can, but does not have to, give away some property to a primary or alternate beneficiary. This clause will begin something like "I make the following specific gifts of personal property, real property, or money . . ."

- *A residuary clause:* Any property not specifically given away is the residue of your estate. The residuary clause gives this away to the residuary beneficiary.

- *A payment of taxes clause:* The executor should be authorized to pay all estate, inheritance, income, and any other applicable taxes that come due after a death.

- *An executor clause:* The executor of the will should be indicated.

- *A guardian clause:* In the event that your spouse predeceases you, or if you and your spouse were to die simultaneously, a guardian for your minor children should be named.

- *A property guardian clause:* As explained in more detail in Chapter 12, "Providing for Children and Parents," a property guardian is someone you can name to oversee the distribution of money and property to your minor children.

- *A children's trust clause:* In addition to, or instead of, a property guardian, establishing a trust fund and naming the trustee for your children in your will is sometimes a good idea.

- *A signing clause:* You must sign the will in the presence of witnesses, and they must sign it in front of you.

- *An affidavit clause:* An affidavit is a statement made under oath that something is true and correct. In this case, it would be that everyone did in fact sign the will in front of each other, and that the testator was competent to make the will.

TYPES OF WILLS. Most people desiring a will need only a basic will, also known as a simple will. It is a will that follows the prerequisites above and either names guardians, leaves money and property to beneficiaries, or both.

A **holographic will** is a will drawn up in your own handwriting, without anyone witnessing it and thereby vouching for the will's authenticity, as is the case with all other wills. Because they are inherently untrustworthy, holographic wills are accepted only in about half of all states.

A testamentary trust will is a variation on a simple will except that it is used to create a trust fund to care for children financially. The advantage to this is that there is a trustee chosen by you who will oversee the use of the trust funds and who often doubles as the guardian.

Spouses who want to ensure that their estate will be litigated for years beyond their death should have a joint will. This is a will made by two people, usually married. It takes both people to change or revoke a joint will, and if any disagreements erupt after it is made, it becomes almost impossible to change or revoke. Furthermore, when one party dies, the remaining party has a very difficult time legally making a new will. All in all, this is a very bad idea.

Videotaped wills are *not permissible in any state* for the same reason that holographic wills are frowned upon—they are easily manipulated and unverifiable. Oral wills are wills that are usually made upon impending death, and are acceptable in only a very few states. Even then, the amount that can be transferred in an oral will is severely restricted. If you want a will, hire an attorney and have a simple will drawn up.

WHAT A WILL CANNOT DO. Although a will is a flexible document that can be used to name guardians and transfer assets through a court-supervised system, there are certain things a will simply, by law, cannot accomplish:

1. *A will cannot disinherit a spouse:* Laws in every state prevent one spouse from attempting to disinherit his mate. Any attempt to do so in a will will be ignored by the court.
2. *A will cannot force a beneficiary to do certain outrageous acts:* Gifts made in a will need not be unconditional. A **conditional bequest** is one in which the beneficiary must *do something* in order to get the money. A condition, like requesting that a son stop smoking, is perfectly fine. What is not fine is a conditional bequest that requests an illegal act ("Henry must kill his dog"), is against public policy ("June must get divorced"), or is impossible to perform ("Jeff must jump from an airplane without a parachute").
3. *A will cannot transfer certain property:* Certain property is transferred automatically at death, and a will cannot change that. Joint tenancy property, property already in a living trust, pay-on-death accounts, life insurance proceeds, and retirement death benefits are among those types of property that cannot be given away in a will.

**The Important Legal Concept to Remember: In certain circumstances, wills make a lot of sense. Valid wills are those that follow the necessary requirements, implement appropriate provisions, and are executed properly.**

# 11

# PROVIDING FOR YOUR SPOUSE

*Put in your will only that which you own*
*Two ways to leave money for your mate*
*Possible problems and some solutions*

When a married person makes a will, he almost always wants to leave the bulk of his estate to his mate. A few precautions need to be made when doing so.

PUT IN YOUR WILL ONLY THAT WHICH YOU OWN. The first thing to remember is that you can give away in your will only that which you own as your separate property. As explained in detail in Chapter 5, "Taking Inventory," much of the property people think they "own" is not really theirs to give away. Either it is co-owned or it is the type of property that cannot be given away in a will. Types of property that *cannot be transferred* in a will include life insurance, pay-on-death accounts, joint tenancy property, and retirement benefits. If you want your spouse to get any of these kinds of property, then he needs to be the named beneficiary.

Another way to ensure that your desired beneficiary gets these kinds of property is to transfer ownership and hold the property in a way that does, in fact, permit you to give it away in your will. For example, title to joint tenancy real estate can be changed to a tenancy in common, and then you can will away your half. A pay-on-death bank account can be changed to a basic savings account in your name alone, and then can be transferred to your spouse, child, or whomever.

Life insurance proceeds transfer automatically at death, no matter what a will has to say about it. The only time life insurance can be given away in a will is when the will creates a trust and the trust is the named beneficiary of the policy.

If you live in one of the nine community property states, you can give away only 50 percent of your community property, since your spouse already owns the other 50 percent. The ten jurisdictions are Arizona, California, Idaho, Louisiana, Nevada, New Mexico, Texas, Washington, Wisconsin, and Puerto Rico.

TWO WAYS TO LEAVE MONEY FOR YOUR MATE. When deciding how to leave property for a spouse, many people opt for the obvious solution—everything to their partner. And that often makes sense. After all, the point of all of this analysis, inventorying, plotting, and planning is usually to make sure that a spouse is provided for.

That, then, is the first and most common option. Leave everything that you own, or the bulk of what you own, outright to your mate with no strings attached. This gives the recipient spouse the freedom to invest the money as he sees fit, use the property, and go about his business with some financial security.

But what if your mate is a poor financial manager? Would it be wise to leave him a sizable estate, or even a modest estate, without some help and guidance? Probably not. Accordingly, the second possibility is to create a **marital support trust** in your will, with your mate named as the beneficiary.

As with all trusts, one of the best features of a marital trust is that you get to name a trusted adviser to help the beneficiary use the money wisely. The trustee can be given as much or as little discretion as warranted for the situation. Conversely, when you leave money for a spouse, or anyone, for that matter (aside from minors), in a will, the money is given without supervision; the recipient can do whatever he wants with it. A trustee can help avoid that.

Great care must be taken when choosing the trustee. You must pick someone whose judgment is trustworthy and who gets along with your mate.

When Tony died, he left behind an estate worth $100,000. Afraid that Liz would squander the money in a few short years, Tony's will left the bulk of his inheritance in trust for Liz, and named his best friend, David, to be cotrustee with Liz.

Liz and David had many disagreements as the years passed. David was very frugal, Liz was not. Although David did a good job of preserving the estate, Liz often had to go without things she wanted. She was sure that Tony would not have wanted this. But because David was the cotrustee, she was forced to abide by his wishes for the rest of her life.

The marital support trust is a flexible tool. It can be generous or frugal. The **principal** in the trust can be used for a spouse's benefit or it can be preserved and given to children after a mate passes away. The options are quite varied, and a marital trust can be tailored to suit your particular needs. (For more information, see Chapter 19, "Subtrusts I: Trusts for Spouses.")

POSSIBLE PROBLEMS AND SOME SOLUTIONS. There are two possible problems when one plans to leave property to a spouse.

The first common problem is the possibility of not leaving enough money for your spouse. If you have an estate worth $200,000, $150,000 of which is your home, then you are leaving your mate only $50,000 with which to live. Under these circumstances, very often, a surviving spouse cannot pay the mortgage yet, needs liquid capital, and is forced to sell the family home in order to survive.

Once again, the solution is life insurance. Although not part of a will, life insurance is part of *any good estate plan*. Term life insurance is inexpensive, and the benefits of having it are tremendous—it provides capital when it is most needed. Getting life insurance is a simple process, and a true act of love.

The second possible problem is the occasion where your present mate is not the parent of your children. If you leave everything in your will to your new mate, there is no guarantee that your children will get any inheritance whatsoever. This is not to say that second spouses are all devious; rather it is merely an acknowledgment of human nature.

The best way to resolve this dilemma is to create in your will a trust for your new husband or wife, but to put limitations on that trust so that when your spouse dies, the money reverts back to your children. This type of marital trust allows you to impose various controls over your property throughout the duration of your spouse's life. Although your spouse gets to use your property while he is alive, when he passes away, the property goes to your children, not his.

Restrictions on this type of trust can include the following:

- Putting money in trust and allowing your spouse to live off the interest only. The principal is reserved for your children.
- Allowing your mate to continue to live in your house during the remainder of his life, but retaining title in the name of the trust.
- Allowing your mate to receive income and dividends from an investment portfolio, but, again, having the trust retain ownership of the portfolio so that it will transfer to your children upon the death of your new husband or wife.

**The Important Legal Concept to Remember: When leaving property for a spouse in a will, make sure to leave enough, and leave it in a way that will make his life easier.**

# 12

# PROVIDING FOR CHILDREN AND PARENTS

*Giving to adult children*
*Taking care of minor children and grandchildren*
*Providing for special needs children*
*Disinheriting a child*
*Protecting a needy parent*

In every state except Louisiana there is no legal requirement necessitating that you leave a child anything in your will. You could decide to leave everything you own to one child, split what you own evenly, or do something in between; it is entirely up to you. While the law on this point may be simple, the execution on your part is usually quite difficult.

GIVING TO ADULT CHILDREN. If your children are adults, you may face a dilemma: should they be treated evenly in your will? There are usually two factors that go into figuring out how much to leave a grown-up child. The first, less problematic, consideration is the quality of your relationship. There is obviously no need, and certainly no legal requirement, that you leave money to a child you have not seen in twenty years. If you do decide to disinherit a child intentionally, see "Disinheriting a Child" (below).

The second issue, usually more perplexing, is need. Adult children often have different financial requirements; one may be a successful doctor, another may be a starving artist. Because an inheritance is a rare opportunity to help a child get ahead, it might make sense to give more to a needy adult child, although the danger of creating bad blood runs high. On the other hand, some parents feel that the successful child should not be penalized for her success. It is a personal and difficult choice to make.

Once you decide how much to leave a child, the question then is, do you leave it to her directly, or with some restrictions? An adult child who has proven to be financially irresponsible might be better served by having the money left in trust, and then allocated by a trustee of your choosing. This type of testamentary trust provision is an easy thing to set up in a will.

TAKING CARE OF MINOR CHILDREN AND GRANDCHILDREN. The first thing to know about leaving money or property to minor children is that they cannot legally own anything, aside from some very small amounts—under $5,000 in most states. There are three legal ways to leave property in your will to your minor child or grandchild:

1. *Appoint a property guardian:* This is different from the "personal guardian" that you name in other parts of your will. A personal guardian raises your child if necessary. A property guardian is your nominee to manage your child's inheritance. Usually it is the same person you name to be the personal guardian, but not always.

Her duties include investing the inherited money wisely, distributing it to your child when needed, and managing the estate properly. The property guardian should be someone who is completely trustworthy. She will also have to report back annually to the probate court to prove that the money is not being squandered or misused. Property guardians often have to post a bond (although many states allow people to waive the bond requirement in their will). In most states, when children turn eighteen the inheritance is theirs with no strings attached.

Being a property guardian is a lot of responsibility, and you should not name someone, or an alternate, without first getting her approval. It is a good idea to leave *explicit instructions* to the guardian as to how you want the money spent. Is the guardian to be liberal or conservative when taking care of the child's financial needs? Should the money be used only for necessities or for extravagances as well? The more your will spells out how you want the money spent, the easier it will be for your guardian to follow your wishes.

2. *Create a custodian account:* Creating a custodian account and naming a custodian is almost always a better choice than naming a property guardian. Property guardians must fill out and submit substantial paperwork and an annual accounting to the probate court yearly. This often requires the assistance of attorneys and/or accountants. Furthermore, the court often severely restricts the discretion of the guardian, and who wants an unknown judge telling your guardian how to raise your child?

None of those problems arise when a custodial account is properly created. The Uniform Transfer to Minors Act (UTMA) permits custodial supervision of money absent court review. It has been adopted by every state except Connecticut, Delaware, Michigan, New York, Pennsylvania, South Carolina, Texas, and Vermont.

Here is how it works: your will needs to have a clause stating that you are making certain bequests (gifts) pursuant to the Uniform Transfer to Minors Act. You then name the amount of the gift, and name a custodian and alternate custodian. Thereafter, your custodian will control and use the property as she sees fit for the benefit of your child. The custodian will have far more discretion than a property guardian, as there is no court supervision and no annual reports to make. The custodianship remains in effect until the child comes of age, which in most states is twenty-one.

That lack of court supervision is both the greatest strength and the weakness of this choice. While court supervision is burdensome, it also can be a useful check to ensure that the custodian is doing her job correctly. If you inherently trust your custodian, as you should, then there is no need for court supervision. If you have some reservations, or are very prudent, naming a property guardian might be a better, yet surely more expensive, way to go.

3. *Establish a trust for your child:* A trust is a private affair. Unlike a will, the contents of your trust are not public, and the trustee is free to do what she thinks is best for your child (within the parameters of your trust document and intentions, of course). Unlike a UTMA gift, there are basically no limits on the length of time that the trust may remain in effect. Most trusts distribute money until the child reaches the age of thirty-five or so.

The trust can be made either before you die (a living trust) or as part of your will (a testamentary trust). Each child can have his or her own trust and trustee (an individual trust) or all children can be covered by one trust (a **family pot trust**).

PROVIDING FOR SPECIAL NEEDS CHILDREN. A will is a very poor tool for helping a mentally or physically disabled child, be he a minor or an adult, since the needs of such children require much planning. Financially, the estate plan must take into account any government assistance the child receives. If the plan is not drawn up correctly, this critical assistance can be lost. Physically, the child will have requirements that necessitate the help of physicians and a personal guardian far beyond the age of eighteen. As a will's primary purpose is to transfer property, these needs are simply not met by the instrument.

A **special needs trust** is a specific kind of trust that is designed and intended to care for special needs children. Government-assistance eligibility can be preserved, and a willing trustee can be named to help the child. (See Chapter 21, "Other Types Of Subtrusts.")

DISINHERITING A CHILD. You are not required by law to leave anything to a child. The key is to make it clear in your will that it is your specific intent to disinherit the child. The most common way is to leave the disavowed child one dollar, and to add a clause stating that it is your specific intent that the child receive no more. Simply leaving the child out of the will is insufficient. This may look to the court like a mistake. Either the child will receive a statutorily mandated share of the estate, or a will contest by the child will likely succeed. (The law on this subject is different in Louisiana, and a resident in that state wanting to disinherit a child will need to consult with an attorney.)

PROTECTING A NEEDY PARENT. None of the restrictions associated with leaving property to minors apply to leaving property to a parent. Adults can receive money and property without limitation. Trust funds too are generally not needed, unless the parent is unable to care for her own affairs, in which case a trust fund and corresponding trustee would be a logical estate-planning choice. Otherwise, you can leave as much of your estate to a parent as you want, provided that you do not illegally disinherit your spouse in the process.

**The Important Legal Concept to Remember: Providing for children takes a lot of foresight, thought, and care. Providing for minors, in particular, is one of the most critical tasks of any estate plan. Although many options exist, setting up a trust for the child is usually the best way to go.**

# 13

# CHOOSING AN EXECUTOR AND A GUARDIAN

*What an executor does*
*Choosing an executor*
*Executor powers*
*Choosing a guardian*

WHAT AN EXECUTOR DOES. The executor of your will is the person charged with carrying out the terms of your will. (If the person you choose is a woman, the term is executrix; in some states the term is personal representative.) It is a very important position of *relatively* limited duration. The operative term is "relatively" because the position lasts as long as your estate is in probate. As a thumbnail rule, a basic estate takes one to two years to probate. Three-year probates and longer are not uncommon, and thus the position may last quite a while indeed.

The executor is not a trustee and is not a guardian. A trustee controls and manages your trust and pays money to the beneficiaries of the trust. Whereas a probate executor's job is completed when probate is over, the trustee of a trust continues in that position indefinitely, until the end of the trust. It is an ongoing position that usually lasts for many years. A personal guardian is the person who will raise your children if need be.

Obviously, it too is a long-term commitment. In contrast, the job of the executor is more *procedural* and limited.

It is the job of the executor to shepherd the case through probate, help determine the legal validity of the will, collect and preserve assets, pay any estate and income taxes that come due, pay creditors, inventory and sell estate property if needed, prepare a final accounting for the court, and, finally, transfer assets to named beneficiaries. It is a job that requires common sense, organization, and perseverance.

> Paul named his eldest daughter, Jillian, to be the executrix of his estate. He trusted Jillian, and knew that she was a competent, organized woman. Although the beginning of the probate was smooth, the IRS soon made a large claim against the estate, as did several business associates of Paul. Two years after Paul died, his estate was still bogged down in probate court. By this time, Jillian's husband had been offered a lucrative position in another city. Jillian moved with him, but was forced to come back every few months to handle the estate's affairs. No one was more relieved than she when the estate finally closed three years after Paul's death.

Although all states have provisions that enable an executor to be reimbursed for his time and expenditures because the job is so time-consuming and detailed, many executors hire a probate attorney or accountant to assist in the completion of the work. Payment of the professional comes out of the estate of the deceased.

To ensure that the executor handles all of these important duties properly, there is a requirement that the executor post a bond. A probate bond is like a bail bond—it is a promise that the bonded person will do what is promised or else the bond company will pay the amount of the bond. This is a bothersome requirement for an executor, usually a friend or family member, who is in essence doing you a favor. Accordingly, many testators have a provision in their will that **waives** the

WILLS   • 6 9

bond requirement, thereby allowing the executor to serve without the bond. If you trust your executor, as you should, your will should waive the need for a bond. Many states have also enacted laws that allow executors to handle most estate issues without court approval, called Independent Administration of Estates acts. It is very wise to specifically permit your executor to handle your affairs under Independent Administration.

CHOOSING AN EXECUTOR. It is both trite and true to say: pick someone you trust. Not only should the person be organized and thorough but she should also be able to work with bereaved family members.

Although it is you who will nominate an executor, it is the court that actually *appoints* the person. The legal requirements are not stringent; the person nominated must be an adult of sound mind. In some states, a convicted felon is prohibited from serving as an executor. It is wise to pick someone who lives near you since probate will occur in the county where you lived at the time of your death.

Most often, people pick spouses or grown children to serve in this capacity. It is good practice to clear your nomination with your intended nominee beforehand as the job is so consuming. It is also good practice to name an alternate.

> After she became a widow, Marge named her sister, Rita, to be the executrix of her estate. Marge lived for another twenty-five years after she made her will, and Rita was eighty-one when Marge died. Rita declined to serve as executrix.

Yes, the chosen person can decline, and if no alternate is named, the court will appoint an executor of its own choosing.

When naming the executor and alternate in your will, be precise. A statement like "I appoint my brother to be the executor of my estate" will cause confusion, and will likely be ignored if you have two brothers. Name names.

EXECUTOR POWERS. The law restricts the powers of an executor to carry out the terms of a will within certain limits. It is therefore often good practice to specifically empower your executor with additional powers. This does not mean that an executor can change the terms of your will. He cannot. But he needs enough power to accomplish the goals you set out. For example:

- *The power to exchange, mortgage, lease, buy, and sell real estate:* It is sometimes necessary to sell an asset of the estate to pay taxes, creditors, or beneficiaries. If not given in the will, the executor will need the permission of the court to do any of these things.

- *The power to employ agents and professionals:* The executor often requires the assistance of an attorney or other professional (e.g., real estate agents, accountants, stockbrokers) to settle the estate.

- *The power to settle claims:* This enables the executor to reach settlements with creditors or other claimants *against* the estate quickly and easily. It also gives the executor the power to resolve claims *on behalf of* the estate.

- *The power to continue business and make investments:* Although the executor has a duty to preserve the estate, including any businesses in the estate, it is best to enumerate these powers in the will. Similarly, it is a good idea to allow the executor the power to make appropriate, prudent investments when necessary (for example, when the estate is taking a long time to settle and money is sitting in a non–interest-bearing account).

- *The power to borrow money:* This is ordinarily needed to compromise claims, pay taxes, or pay creditors.

CHOOSING A GUARDIAN. Is there a more important decision you will make in your lifetime? Maybe not. If you are married, you need to name your spouse as the guardian should you die since he would be anyway, by law. The real issue is, who will be the alternate, or who will the guardian be in the unlikely event that you and your spouse were to die at the same time? Similarly, if you are a single parent, the decision of who will raise your minor children in your absence is of the utmost importance.

No one will raise your children like you would, but who will come closest? Who shares your values? Who is stable financially, physically, emotionally? Who will love your children and make them feel special? Who will honor you and your wishes?

When making this decision, the financial status of the proposed guardian should not be a major concern. Utilizing methods discussed throughout this book, such as life insurance, children's trusts, and property guardians, it should be clear that there are many ways to provide for your child financially in your absence.

Again, make sure that you discuss your desire with your designated guardian. This is not the type of thing one springs upon someone without express prior approval. An unwanted guardian designation and the corresponding crisis atmosphere could prove to be devastating to your children at a time when they are most vulnerable.

It is also very smart not only to name a guardian but to leave that person explicit directions as to how you want your child raised. These instructions can cover education, religion, care, responsibility, or any other matter of importance to you.

Sue's will stated: "I hereby name my brother Robert to be the guardian of my minor children. I direct my guardian to raise my children in the Catholic faith. Above all, I want school and good grades stressed when raising my children."

Directions can be very explicit and lengthy. Aside from explicit instructions, the best plan of action is to sit down periodically with your chosen guardian and explain how things are going with the kids. Tell him what you want done, what each needs, and how you want them raised. This, above all, will give your guardian a good idea of how you want your children brought up.

**The Important Legal Concept to Remember: Naming an executor and guardian should be well-thought-out decisions. The ability to have your assets transferred successfully, and the lives of your children, depend on the quality of these decisions.**

# WILL CONTESTS

*Grounds for contesting a will*
*How to prevent a will contest*
*How to contest a will successfully*

GROUNDS FOR CONTESTING A WILL. Anyone who has an "interest" in a will may contest its validity. Not everyone, however, has an interest. As a general rule, an interested person is someone who is an heir, or who was named in a previous will. A friend who was never named in a will, and who would not inherit anything by law if the will were disregarded, is not an interested person and cannot legally contest the will. Similarly, stepchildren and ex-spouses cannot usually contest a will.

Most wills are not contested, and few contests are successful. This is so for a couple of reasons. First, in many states, the challenger usually has only a few months after the deceased passes away to initiate the will contest. By the time the will is admitted into probate and the assets of the estate are established, the window to challenge the will by the disgruntled heir may have closed.

More often, will contests are unsuccessful because the grounds for a challenge are really quite limited. There are only five reasons to contest a will, and one of those reasons *is not* unfairness. The absolute only person who can challenge a will based on unfairness is a spouse who was not left her legal share of the estate. Otherwise, the only grounds for contesting a will are

1. *Lack of* **testamentary capacity***:* The testator (i.e., the maker of the will) must be of sound mind at the time she makes the will. She must know and understand what she is signing and what the document purports to do. If, at the time she signed the will, the testator lacked this so-called "testamentary capacity," a will contest is proper.

2. *Lack of volitional consent:* The testator must make the will by her own choice and decision. If there was duress (i.e., if someone such as a spouse or lawyer exerted too much pressure on the testator to make the will a certain way), then the will was not made voluntarily and is invalid. Similarly, if someone defrauded the testator into making the will, there was no volitional consent.

3. *Improper execution of the will:* The will must be signed by the testator in front of the proper number of witnesses, and then signed by them.

4. *Revocation:* A will can be contested on the grounds that it was previously revoked by the testator.

5. *Forgery:* Any kind of false will, be it through forgery or other means, is contestable.

HOW TO PREVENT A WILL CONTEST: The key to drafting a will that will not be contested is to add a **no-contest clause** in it, although "no-contest" is a bit of a misnomer. The clause does not actually forbid will contests; what it does is make any contest a very risky endeavor for the contester. The effect of a no-contest clause is to give the person challenging the will nothing if the challenge is unsuccessful.

Ruth's will left almost everything in her $100,000 estate to her daughter Anne, although it did leave $5,000 to her other daughter, Irene. In order to prevent a contest of the will by Irene, Ruth had inserted into the will a sentence that read: "Should this will be unsuccessfully contested, the person bringing the contest is to receive nothing from my estate."

Irene had two choices. If she did contest the will, she would get either another $45,000 or $0. If she did not contest the will, she would be guaranteed $5,000. Because Irene could find nothing to contest in how the will was made, and because unfairness is no grounds to contest a will, Irene opted not to contest the document, and begrudgingly took her $5,000.

Aside from a no-contest clause, there are two other ways to prevent a will contest. The first is to enter into an agreement with the beneficiary during your life whereby the beneficiary agrees not to contest the will in exchange for certain other benefits. This is most commonly used between spouses when they sign prenuptial agreements. Such agreements often state that neither party will contest the will of the other.

The second method is to videotape the execution of the will. This is especially appropriate if you are older and suspect that an unhappy heir may challenge your will on the grounds that you were not competent to execute it. The videotape can document your sound mind.

HOW TO CONTEST A WILL SUCCESSFULLY. First, anyone wishing to contest a will must be an interested person. Second, there must be grounds for objection; meritless contesters are often monetarily sanctioned by the court.

Assuming, then, that you think you have valid grounds to contest a will, the first step is to hire competent counsel. Legal procedure is a maze, and probate procedure is the crown jewel of legal mazes. Do not delay. In most states, you have only a few months, and sometimes less than a month, within which to file a contest.

Once your attorney has timely filed the challenge, probate will ground to a halt. There is a strategic value to this. Since everything stops while the contest is being litigated, and since beneficiaries are usually anxious to get their inheritance, a will contest of even dubious merit *can often result in a cash settlement so as to keep the probate on track.* Thus, merely initiating a will contest sometimes results in a small, quick settlement (as long as there are ostensible grounds to contest the will).

If your goal is to get a larger share of an estate you feel is rightly yours, you will need to litigate the matter to the end. Be prepared to spend many thousands of dollars and many years to get to a resolution.

**The Important Legal Concept to Remember: Will contests occur on television more often than in real life. A potential will contest is a fairly easy problem for a good estate planner to avoid, and contesting a will is rarely a successful act.**

# CHANGING OR REVOKING YOUR WILL

*When to make a new will*

*When and how to change your existing will*

*How to revoke your will*

WHEN TO MAKE A NEW WILL. Small changes to your will can be accomplished by changing your present will (see below). Examples include adding a specific gift for someone or changing an alternate beneficiary. On the other hand, certain events in your life necessitate writing a new will altogether. These events are

- *Getting divorced:* Since most wills leave the bulk of the estate assets to the spouse, when you get divorced you need to write a new will so that your ex-spouse won't be able to get the property at your death that she wasn't able to get in the divorce.
- *Getting married:* In many states, exchanging vows has the dual effect of not only creating marriage but also revoking prior wills. Remember that a will that does not provide for a spouse illegally disinherits that spouse. Therefore, marriage often has the effect of revoking, by law, previous wills. If you get married, get a new will.

- *New children:* Even though all states have laws that give children born or adopted after the making of a will a share of the estate even if they were not mentioned in the will (called **pretermitted heir statutes**), it is far better to rewrite your will when a new child enters the family.

- *Newly acquired property:* A major change, for better or worse, in your assets requires a new will to dispose of the property accordingly. If you do not change your will, and you do acquire new property, it will pass to the residuary beneficiary. If that is acceptable to you, there is no need for a new will.

- *Moving to a different state:* If you move from a common law state to a community property state, or vice versa, your will must be revised to account for the difference in state laws. Note, however, that if you move from one common law state to another, or from one community property state to another, then a will that was valid in the first state will also likely be valid in the new state.

- *Death of a beneficiary, executor, or guardian:* The death of any of these three important entities should prompt you to make a new will.

WHEN AND HOW TO CHANGE YOUR EXISTING WILL. A change to your existing will should be accomplished by having a codicil drafted. A codicil is simply an addition or modification to an existing will. It may add, subtract, modify, or even revoke provisions of an existing will. Codicils are best used to make small changes to a will.

Randy made his will when he was in his late forties. His will left half of his estate to his brother, and the other half to his sister. When he was sixty, Randy married. He had a codicil written up stating that his wife was to receive his entire estate. Although he died a year later, his wife, brother, and sister fought for another four years over who was to inherit Randy's estate since the will and the codicil were mutually exclusive.

There is simply too much room for confusion, and therefore expensive litigation, when large changes in the will are made by a codicil.

If you do want to use a codicil, you must do so correctly. Merely writing in the change on your will is insufficient. Just as the formalities for a will must accompany the making of a valid will, so too must these formalities be followed when making an enforceable codicil. And the reason is the same: wills are important; codicils are important. Courts want assurance that the will or codicil reflects the true intention of the testator. Formalities and proper execution provide this assurance.

Therefore, to change your will by codicil, the codicil must be typed or word-processed, dated, and signed in front of two disinterested witnesses (three in some states), and the witnesses must attest to the signing of the codicil.

HOW TO REVOKE YOUR WILL. If you want to cancel your present will (called revoking your will), there are two ways to do so.

The first and probably most common method is to have a new will made up that specifically revokes any previous wills. One of the very first clauses in almost any will is a sentence that reads something like "This will specifically revokes all prior wills made by me." Revoking a will by this type of subsequent writing is the preferred method of revocation as it guarantees that you will still have a will after the previous one is revoked.

The second, less preferred method is to physically destroy the previous will. As indicated, the problem with this method is that you will likely be without a will after you destroy the first one. If you do choose this method, it is necessary to damage, destroy, or alter the *actual words* that make up the will. Writing "REVOKED" in the margins of the will will not do, since the *words* themselves are not touched by the alteration. Writing "REVOKED" over the words on the first page will do, as will tearing up the will.

And remember: if you get married, your present will may be revoked as a matter of law.

The Important Legal Concept to Remember: The critical factor when deciding to change a will is the degree of change in your life necessitating the modification. Big changes mean new wills. Small changes mean codicils properly executed.

# 16

# A TYPICAL WILL

The following is a sample will, but you are cautioned that different states have different requirements as to what must be in a will, and individual circumstances dictate different types of wills.

Phil and Mindy had been married for twenty-five years when Phil passed away. Phil and Mindy had three children, Jillian, Sydney, and Mara, although only Mara was still living at home when Phil died. Phil and Mindy owned a home together as tenants in common that was paid for and was worth $100,000. Phil also had $150,000 in separate assets. Phil left the following will:

ARTICLE I:
RECITATIONS

1. I, Phil Sobel, a resident of Eugene, Oregon, being of sound mind and memory, being of the age of majority, and not acting under duress, menace, fraud, or undue influence, declare this to be my will. *[Already, Phil is attempting to preclude a will contest.]*

2. *Revocation:* I hereby revoke all prior wills and codicils that I have previously made. *[This clause is very important. By revoking all prior wills and codicils, Phil is ensuring that there will be*

*no mistake that this is his intended will. Any earlier-dated will would be ignored by the probate court.]*

3. *Marital Status:* I am now married. My wife's name is Mindy Sobel. *[If Phil gets divorced, he will need to rewrite this will since Mindy gets most of his estate.]*

4. *Children:* I have the following living children:

| NAME | DATE OF BIRTH |
|------|---------------|
| A. Jillian Sobel | 1/4/72 |
| B. Sydney Sobel | 9/11/73 |
| C. Mara Sobel | 3/14/85 |

ARTICLE II:
EXECUTOR, AND POWERS OF THE EXECUTOR

5. I hereby name Larry Diego to be the executor of my estate. Should Larry Diego not be able to serve, for whatever reason, I name Spencer Diego to be the executor of my estate. The executor shall serve without bond. *[Phil names both a primary and an alternate executor. In order to make their job easier, he states that whoever the executor is, no bond is needed.]*

6. I hereby give my executor the following powers: *[Phil wants to make sure that the executor has enough power to settle the estate and get Phil's money to his wife and kids. Therefore, and because Phil trusts his executor, Phil gives his executor broad powers.]*

A. I authorize my executor to pay all of my funeral expenses from the estate.

B. The executor shall have and take all powers necessary to probate this will, including filing a petition in the appropriate court.

C. I grant the executor the following powers, to be used at his discretion, for the orderly administration of my estate:

1. To do all acts which may become necessary to carry out the terms of my will and to probate my estate;

B. My child is to be taught personal responsibility;

C. My child is to be given much love and positive encouragement;

D. My child is to go to college.

*[The four directions above were very important to Phil, although these directions could have been far more detailed if he so wanted. Of everyone he knew, Phil decided that it was his family who could best raise his minor daughter as he would want her to be raised. Notice that the money needed to carry out his wishes is not discussed here; it is dealt with in the "Trust" section below.]*

8. *Property Guardian:* If a property guardian is needed, I name my brother Stanley Sobel as the property guardian, to serve without bond. If this person is unwilling or unable to serve as property guardian, I name my sister Robyn Natalia as property guardian to serve without bond. *[Mara may end up with property that Phil cannot anticipate when making the will. This section, then, is merely precautionary]*

ARTICLE IV:
SPECIFIC GIFTS

9. I leave to my daughter Jillian $25,000, to be held in the Children's Trust, created below. If Jillian does not survive me, then the $25,000 shall revert to the residuary of my estate. *[If Jillian passes away before Phil, the $25,000 will become part of the remainder of Phil's estate, which is given to Mindy (see below).]*

10. I leave to my daughter Sydney $25,000, to be held in the Children's Trust, created below. If Sydney does not survive me, then the $25,000 shall revert to the residuary of my estate.

11. I leave to my daughter Mara $25,000, to be held in the Children's Trust, created below. If Mara does not survive me, then the $25,000 shall revert to the residuary of my estate.

2. To pay all enforceable debts and taxes that may come due or be claimed against the estate;

3. To resolve and settle all claims both for and against my estate;

4. To sell, lease, and/or encumber real property as needed to prudently administer my estate;

5. To retain and control property;

6. To retain, continue, run, and/or dissolve any business which is part of my estate as needed to prudently administer my estate;

7. To convert stock, notes, bonds, and/or other securities for the benefit of my estate.

8. To resolve my estate under the applicable Independent Administration of Estates act.

The powers granted to my executor in this section are in addition to the power and authority granted to executors by law. It is my intent that my executor be given broad discretion to settle, resolve, and/or administer my estate without court supervision.


ARTICLE III:

GUARDIANS

7. *Personal Guardian:* If my wife does not survive me, I name my brother Stanley Sobel as the personal guardian of my minor child, Mara, to serve without bond. *[If Mindy does survive Phil, no guardian is needed.]* If this person is unwilling or unable to serve as personal guardian, I name my sister Robyn Natalia to be the personal guardian and to serve without bond.

The personal guardian of my child is to take the following directions into account when raising my minor child or children:

A. My child is to be raised in the Jewish faith;

ARTICLE V:
RESIDUARY ESTATE

12. I leave the rest, residue, and remainder of my estate, that is, all of the property not otherwise disposed of by this will, to my wife, Mindy Sobel. If she does not survive me, I give my residuary estate to the Children's Trust created by this will in Article VI, below. *[Mindy gets the bulk of Phil's estate unless she dies first, in which case the kids will get it all through the trust. Note too that Phil may have left other property to Mindy, such as life insurance or pay-on-death bank accounts, which are not transferred by a will.]*

ARTICLE VI:
CHILDREN'S TRUST

*[Because Phil has one child who is a minor and two who are young adults, he does not want to leave money to them outright. Instead, he wants to leave money for them that can be supervised by someone. By creating a trust, Phil can select a trustee to oversee the money left to his children and ensure that it will be spent wisely. As you can see, creating a trust is a fairly easy thing to do.]*

13. I hereby create the Sobel Children's Trust (the "Trust") for my living children (the "beneficiaries.") All property left for my children in this will shall be held for them in this one Trust.

14. Each of my children who is living at the time of my death will be a beneficiary of this Trust.

15. I name my wife, Mindy, to be the trustee of the Trust, to serve without bond. If Mindy is unable or unwilling to serve, I name my brother Stanley to be the successor trustee, to serve without bond.

16. The trustee shall use the Trust assets for the benefit of the beneficiaries. The trustee may use both the income and the principal of the Trust as she or he sees fit for the health, wel-

fare, support, maintenance, or education of the beneficiaries. *[The trustee has broad latitude to use the money as he or she thinks is best for the benefit of the beneficiaries.]*

17. Any sums in the Trust left by this will for a beneficiary not already spent on a beneficiary by the time the beneficiary reaches the ages listed below shall be distributed to that beneficiary as follows:

    A. One third of the remaining principal and interest of each child's share shall be given to each child outright when the child reaches the age of twenty-five. *[Each of the three children will receive 33 percent of her remaining money (that is, the money not yet spent on her) when she reaches the age of twenty-five, another 33 percent at age thirty, and the remaining 33 percent at age thirty-five.]*

    B. One third of the remaining principal and interest of each child's share shall be given to each child outright when the child reaches the age of thirty.

    C. One third of the remaining principal and interest of each child's share shall be given to each child outright when the child reaches the age of thirty-five.

    Any sums not distributed to a beneficiary shall be kept by the trustee, added to the remaining principal of the Trust, and distributed pursuant to this section.

18. Aside from other powers given to the trustee by this Trust, the trustee shall also have the power to invest the Trust principal prudently, hire professional advisers as needed, and shall have all such other powers granted to trustees by the laws of this state. *[The trustee will have the ability to administer the trust as needed.]*

19. This Trust shall be administered without court supervision. The beneficiaries cannot transfer or assign their rights under this Trust. *[None of the children can sell her share of the trust, as most beneficiaries can.]* Any clause of this Trust deemed by a court of law to be unenforceable or invalid shall be severable from the rest of the Trust and shall not

cause the remainder of the Trust to be invalid. *[If any section of the trust is found invalid, for some reason, the remainder of the trust will still be enforceable.]*

20. This Trust shall end upon the occurrence of any of the following:

   A. With respect to any individual beneficiary, the Trust shall end as to that beneficiary when she reaches the age of thirty-five.

   B. The Trust is depleted through distributions as provided for in this Trust document. *[If necessary, the trust may use up all trust funds before Mara reaches the age of thirty-five. If so, that's it.]*

<br>

ARTICLE VII:
MISCELLANEOUS

21. If my wife and I die under such circumstances that the order of our deaths cannot be easily determined, my wife shall be deemed to have died before me. *[This clause accomplishes an important goal. If Phil dies together with Mindy, and it is determined that he died a minute before she did, then Mindy would inherit the bulk of Phil's estate for that one minute she outlived him. Thereafter, all of his belongings would pass to whomever Mindy chose in her will. This clause prevents that. It ensures that Phil's intended beneficiaries get what he left them, and because Mindy has the same clause in her will, her beneficiaries get what she left them.]*

22. I have purposely made no provision for any person not heretofore mentioned in this will, whether claiming to be an heir of mine or not. If any person, named in this will or not, shall unsuccessfully contest this will or object to any provisions thereof, I give to that person so contesting NOTHING in lieu of any provision which I may have made or which I have made herein for such person so contesting or objecting. *[A typical no-contest clause.]*

SIGNATURE

I sign my name to this will on this 4th day of April, 1996, at Eugene, Oregon, and affirm that this is my will, which I make freely and voluntarily.

Phil Sobel

WITNESSES

*[The legal formalities and execution needed to create a valid will are attested to in this section. Phil is of legal age, and of sound mind and memory. He voluntarily signed and dated the will in front of the necessary number of witnesses, and they signed and dated it in front of each other and Phil.]*

Each of the undersigned, on oath, states:

The attached will was signed by Phil Sobel, the testator named in the will, on the 4th day of April, 1996, at his home, 1800 Mariposa Lane, Eugene, Oregon.

Each of us observed the signing of the will by Phil Sobel and each of us then signed the will at the request of Phil Sobel, in his presence, and in the presence of each other. Phil Sobel, at the time he signed this will, and to the best of our knowledge, was over the age of eighteen years, and of sound mind and memory, and not under any restraint, duress, incapacity, or in any respect incompetent to make a will. Each of us is now over the age of eighteen years and a competent witness.

We declare under penalty of perjury that the foregoing is true and correct, and that this Affidavit was signed on this 4th day of April 1996, at Eugene, Oregon.

(NAME)                              (SIGNATURE)

(ADDRESS)

(NAME)                 (SIGNATURE)

(ADDRESS)

(NAME)                 (SIGNATURE)

(ADDRESS)

The Important Legal Concept to Remember: When making a will, it is critical to execute it properly and follow all formalities and legal requirements. Within that context, you can pretty much say and do anything you want.

# LIVING TRUSTS

# 17

# LIVING TRUSTS MADE EASY

*What is a revocable living trust?*

*What a living trust can do*

*What a living trust cannot do*

*Steps in getting a trust*

*How to provide for your family*

WHAT IS A REVOCABLE LIVING TRUST? A living trust is nothing more than a document that creates a separate legal entity, set up by you, owned by you, and controlled by you, that holds your property for your benefit. *Because this "entity" owns your property, when you die there is nothing to probate.* But because you own and control the trust, you maintain control of your property throughout your life. Then, upon your death, the trust transfers your property to whomever you want, just as a will would.

It helps to think of a trust as a container. When you own property without a trust, it's as if you hold your property in your hands. When you own property with a trust, you still hold your property, but now you hold it in your container. That's it. When you pass away, the contents of the container can be retained for use by others, or can be distributed to whomever you wish.

This container is similar to a corporation, but with some significant differences. A corporation is nothing more than a separate legal entity set up by real people to conduct business. It is the corporation that owns property at the behest of the people who formed it. Like a corporation, your trust is your own separate legal entity that you set up to own your property. And because it's your trust and you are the trustee, you control and use your property however you wish.

A living trust is really quite a simple thing to create and own. It need not be intimidating. It need not be complex. It need not change how you use and control your property in any manner whatsoever. It is nothing more than a container created by you to hold your property for your use while you are alive, and then a mechanism to transfer that property to whom you want after you pass away without court supervision.

Dario and Jessica owned a home, some financial investments, two cars, and lots of furniture. Without a trust, they owned the property, and upon their death, all of their property went through probate. Had they created a living trust during their lifetimes, although their trust would have owned all of this property, they could have used any asset in any manner they wished. Upon their death, there would have been no probate.

It is called a *living* trust because you create it while you are alive for use during your lifetime. Conversely, a trust created in your will (and, therefore, which comes into effect only when you die) is called a *testamentary* trust. As such, it fails to accomplish one of the main objectives of a living trust—the ability to circumvent probate.

It is called a *revocable* living trust because after it is made, you (called, alternatively, the **trust maker**, grantor, settlor, or trustor) can always change it. You can add or delete assets, alter beneficiaries, or revoke the entire trust altogether if you so choose.[1] An *irrevocable* trust is just that—irrevocable. It can-

---

[1] Hereinafter, when the term "living trust" is used in this book, it means a revocable living trust, unless otherwise specified.

not be changed after it comes into existence. An asset transferred into an irrevocable trust container becomes the asset of the trust *forever* and *cannot* be retrieved. An irrevocable living trust cannot later be changed and is therefore usually a bad idea (although irrevocable life insurance trusts and irrevocable **charitable remainder trusts** *are* a good idea—see Chapter 21, "Other Types of Subtrusts.")

It is easy to get confused by living trusts because they are often combined with other ongoing subtrusts to accomplish various estate-planning goals. Some people are not sure where the living trust ends and the subtrusts begin. The main thing to understand is this: the main document used in trust estate planning is the living trust. It is the basis from which all other trusts may spring. After a living trust is created, it may also create different subtrusts, but these subtrusts are distinct and different from the basic living trust. The living trust is your tool for your life. The subtrusts are offshoots you create for the benefit of *others*. For example, a living trust can be used to avoid probate, and ongoing trusts can be added to take care of children or save on estate taxes.

WHAT A LIVING TRUST CAN DO. Obviously, one of the main advantages of a living trust is that it allows your assets to transfer to your beneficiaries without probate. Other advantages are equally significant. Because it is a private document that avoids court oversight, a living trust also protects your privacy and that of your loved ones. No one aside from your beneficiaries and trustee will ever know the size of your estate and to whom you left it.

If the value of your estate is more than $600,000, then an equally important aspect of living trust estate planning is the potential tax savings when the proper types of subtrusts are created.

Another very important aspect of a living trust is its ability to protect you in the case of a disability. If, for example, you have only a will and you become disabled, your spouse or child will have to go to court to have a conservator appointed to oversee your affairs. The wheels of justice grind slowly; it will take considerable time and money for a conservator to be appointed. By utilizing a living trust, your successor trustee or cotrustee can oversee your affairs without court approval if you become incapacitated. Health-care decisions can also be made in advance. (See Chapter 28, "Planning for a Disability.")

A living trust that incorporates a children's subtrust can also enable you to care for your children financially after you are gone, be they minors or adults. Without a trust, your property transfers to your children at the age of twenty-one (usually). With a trust, you can name a trustee to oversee the distribution of your estate to your children at various intervals, or as needed, depending upon your intention and the needs of your kids.

> In his living trust, Sam created a "Children's Trust" for his two adult sons. The Children's Trust named Sam's brother as trustee. It also specified that each son was to receive his share of the inheritance in three phases: one-third at the age of twenty-five, one-third at the age of thirty, and the final third at thirty-five. Although both sons squandered their first two gifts, by the time each turned thirty-five, they used their money wisely.

WHAT A LIVING TRUST CANNOT DO. A living trust cannot name a guardian for small children; only a will can do that. A living trust cannot put assets into your trust that were not put into the trust before your death; only a **pour-over will** or a power of attorney can do that.

A living trust cannot protect your assets from creditors. While you are alive, your creditors have an equal right to get at your assets in trust as they would if you had no trust at all; the trust *does not* protect your assets from creditors during your life. And after your death, one of the few areas where wills surpass trusts is in creditors' rights. After you die, your creditors have roughly six months to make claims against your estate in probate, while they have usually twelve months to do so against an estate transferred through a trust.

Importantly, the many tax benefits available through proper trust planning are not part of any bare-bones living trust. Special tax-savings subtrusts must be created in addition to your living trust in order to get this benefit.

STEPS IN GETTING A TRUST. Despite these few flaws, getting a living trust is advisable, and really a fairly simple thing to do. There are basically three parts to creating a living trust.

First, the trust must be drafted. This means going to a lawyer and having a trust drawn up. Although any trust should be tailored to suit individual circumstances, all trusts must contain the following provisions:

1. *A trustee must be named:* This is the person who controls the trust and trust property. While you are alive, you should be the trustee.

2. *A successor trustee must be named:* This is the person who will transfer the trust property to your beneficiaries after you pass away. The successor trustee is also the person who will manage your affairs should you become incapacitated during your life.

3. *Beneficiaries of the trust must be named:* These are the people who will get your property after you die.

4. *Property held by the trust must be named:* Property held by the trust should be named in the trust.

5. *Terms of the trust must be specified:* Instructions as to how the trust is to be carried out must be specified.

Second, property to be held by the trust must be transferred to the trust. After you have the trust drafted, you will need to transfer ownership of your property to the trust in order for the trust to have any effect. A trust without property is *completely useless.* Creating a trust without funding it is like getting a glass of water without putting water in it. It is a pointless exercise. Chapter 23, "Funding Your Trust," explains how to transfer your property into your trust.

Finally, after the trust is made and funded, it must be managed. During your life, while you (or you and your spouse) are the trustee, you will manage and control the trust. You will continue to use your property as you wish, be able to buy and sell property, and alter or change the trust however you want. Your tax liabilities will not change because of the trust and will continue to be paid by you as if you had no trust at all. Upon your death, your successor trustee will manage the trust pursuant to your instructions contained within the trust.

HOW TO PROVIDE FOR YOUR FAMILY. The important thing to remember about a living trust is that alone it is nothing more than a **will substitute**. All it really does is transfer your property to your loved ones, just as a will would. The main difference is that it is does so privately, and without probate. However, without anything more, a bare-bones living trust terminates after the property is given away, creates no long-term protection for your family, nor does it implement the tax savings for which living trusts are known.

Yet it is very easy to create these financial protections in your living trust. All you need to do is have the proper subtrust made part of your living trust (subtrusts are also sometimes called ongoing trusts because they last longer than the original living trust). An ongoing subtrust is nothing more than a trust within your trust that takes effect and continues on after you pass away.

The benefits of subtrusts are threefold. First, keeping in mind that federal estate taxes do not start until the value of an estate is more than $600,000, a subtrust can save on estate taxes for estates worth more than that amount. Second, a subtrust can financially care for children by utilizing the proper kind of children's trust. Third, a subtrust will allow you to have a trustee control the distribution of the trust assets. *The real*

*magic of living trusts comes when the right subtrusts are made part
of your overall living trust.*

There are many different types of subtrusts. Most ongoing
subtrusts take effect upon the death of the grantor, and last for
a specific period of time, say, until a child graduates college or
some other specific event or amount of time. An ongoing trust
usually can last no longer than one generation. The main subtrusts are as follows:

- *Bypass trusts:* These are also known as A-B trusts and marital support trusts. A bypass subtrust is one designed to protect a spouse and save on estate taxes for estates worth more
  than $600,000. (See Chapter 19, "Trusts for Spouses.")
- *Children's trusts:* There are three types of children's trusts.
  Family pot trusts are subtrusts in which a lump sum is left
  for all children, and the trustee oversees the dispersal of
  that money in accordance with your wishes. Individual
  trusts are used to provide each child with her own specific
  trust. Special needs trusts help care for disabled children.
  (See Chapter 20, "Children's Trusts.")
- *Other trusts:* Charitable remainder trusts are trusts created
  to leave substantial amounts of money to charity. Irrevocable
  life insurance trusts (ILITs) can be used to leave life insurance for your beneficiaries tax-free.

**The Important Legal Concept to Remember: Living trusts
are almost always the best way to plan your estate. When
children, spouses, taxes, or charity are a concern, specific
subtrusts can be combined with the main living trust to
accomplish specific goals.**

# 18

# HOW A BASIC LIVING TRUST WORKS

*How it works if you are married*
*How it works if you are single*

## HOW IT WORKS IF YOU ARE MARRIED.

Jim and Elizabeth have an estate worth about $500,000, consisting of their home, various financial investments, a time-share condo, and two cars. Jim and Elizabeth have two adult children.

Because the value of their estate is under the magic number of $600,000, Jim and Elizabeth do not have to worry about potential estate taxes. However, probate should be a definite concern when they plan their estate. The first probate, consisting of half the total estate ($250,000), at 8 percent, would cost their children $20,000. The second probate would cost $18,400 (since the probate fees of $20,000 would have been deducted from the other $250,000.)

Jim and Elizabeth created the "Jim and Elizabeth Living Trust." They transferred all of their assets, real estate, cars, and all into the trust, and named themselves as trustees. The trust states that after both parents pass away, the successor trustee (Jim's brother) is to distribute the remaining funds to the two kids immediately. Three years after the trust was set up, Jim passed away.

After Jim died, and because his wife was a cotrustee with Jim, Elizabeth retained use and control of all their assets. Furthermore, because they had previously transferred all their property into the trust, there was no probate for Jim's estate. When Elizabeth dies, because the estate assets are still in trust, there is again nothing to probate. Jim's brother thereafter would distribute the remaining assets to Jim and Elizabeth's two children.

After Jim died, Elizabeth became progressively incapacitated. Jim's brother had to admit her into a convalescent home. He paid her medical bills with "Jim and Elizabeth trust" funds, and took care of all other business until Elizabeth died. He then distributed the remaining $100,000 to the two kids.

By creating a living trust, Jim and Elizabeth avoided the time and expense of two probates. Furthermore, the trust allowed Jim's brother to care for Elizabeth without the time and expense of a court-mandated conservatorship proceeding. Jim and Elizabeth also kept their finances private, retained control of their property, and helped their children.

## HOW IT WORKS IF YOU ARE SINGLE.

Adam owns his home, a mutual fund, checking and savings accounts, and a car. The value of his estate, including life insurance, is roughly $100,000. Adam has one child, a son, age ten.

Because the value of his estate is under $600,000, Adam does not have to worry about potential estate taxes. Avoiding probate and taking care of his son are his main concerns. If Adam chooses to have a will, his estate is assured of going through probate. Assuming 8 percent will go toward probate fees and costs, Adam can expect that $8,000 of his estate will go to strangers instead of his son. With a living trust, Adam can make sure that this money will instead go to his child.

Adam's trust will name himself as trustee and primary beneficiary, and will also name a successor trustee. Adam will need to transfer all of his assets into the trust. During his life, Adam will retain control of all of his assets.

A basic living trust ends soon after the death of the settlor. The successor trustee distributes the assets and that's it. Because he has a minor child, Adam needs to have his trust last a bit longer. He can do so by simply having a subtrust added into his living trust, often called an A trust, which states that the successor trustee is to continue to use the trust assets to care for the child. The living trust is Adam's trust. The A trust is the son's trust. It is very simple.

When he dies, Adam's estate will pass directly to his successor trustee without having to go through probate. Thereafter, the successor trustee will hold and use the property for Adam's son, pursuant to the instructions left by Adam in his trust.

Adam created a living trust, and named his sister as the successor trustee. His trust states that after Adam's death, the trust funds should be used to care for all of his son's needs and pay for his college education. The remainder, if any, should be distributed to his son when he turns thirty.

As a result of creating a simple revocable living trust, Adam was able to control his property during his life, keep his affairs private, avoid probate, and have someone financially care for his son until he became an adult.

**The Important Legal Concept to Remember: Living trusts can do a lot more than simply save taxes. They can achieve a variety of estate-planning goals, including retaining privacy and avoiding probate, along with its associated length and fees.**

# 19

# SUBTRUSTS I: TRUSTS FOR SPOUSES

*Marital trusts*

*Bypass trusts*

*The mechanics of how a bypass trust works*

*Restrictions on a bypass trust*

Most spouses create joint living trusts. Even if property is technically owned separately because of state law, most couples married for any length of time consider all property jointly owned. It would be twice as expensive and equally cumbersome for a married couple to create and fund two separate living trusts when the goal of each is usually the same: to care for the spouse and children. Accordingly, joint living trusts among married partners is the norm.

MARITAL TRUSTS. It is often preferable to leave an inheritance for a spouse in trust rather than outright. There are several reasons for this. As always, money or property left in trust completely avoids probate. But there are even more compelling reasons. Leaving property in trust allows a husband and wife to keep their affairs totally private. It allows a spouse to get help from the trustee. It also gives a spouse an "excuse" to say no— "I can't lend you that kind of money, it's tied up in the trust." Maybe the most important reason is that it can keep your spouse's creditors from taking trust property, and it can do so while giving the spouse full access to the trust funds.

A **marital trust** is simple to create. It is nothing more than a certain type of subtrust created within your living trust. As such, all one needs to do is have the marital trust made part of the living trust document, specify what property is to go into the subtrust upon one's death, and name a trustee. The trustee may be the same as the successor trustee or not.

The trust will take effect only after you pass away. When you do pass away, your living trust will fund the new subtrust with whatever assets you leave to your mate. Your instructions can be very liberal, allowing your mate ample access to the trust money, or it can be very conservative. It all depends on your goals. Upon the death of your spouse, all property left in the marital trust will avoid probate.

You can and should have a spendthrift clause added to this subtrust. This clause tells the trustee that the trust property can never be used to pay your spouse's creditors. By so doing, your mate will be able to use and enjoy the money without having to worry that her creditors will be able to reach her inheritance. Spendthrift clauses are permissible in most states. Note, though, that a spendthrift clause can work only for others; you cannot shield your own money from your creditors by putting such a clause in your living trust.

BYPASS TRUSTS. A bypass trust is another sort of subtrust of your living trust. While the main advantage of a normal living trust is the avoidance of probate, the main advantage of a bypass trust is the ability to care for a spouse while legally *avoiding estate taxes*.

Because people with estates under $600,000 do not need to worry about federal estate taxes, the only ones who need concern themselves with creating a tax-saving bypass trust are those couples whose estates exceed this amount. Unmarried couples can use a bypass trust just as easily as married partners although there is usually no need for one if you are single.

The tax savings achieved by creating a bypass trust within your living trust can be significant. For example, an estate worth $800,000 will pay *approximately $40,000* in estate taxes without a bypass trust. That same estate with a bypass trust incorporated as part of the estate plan will pay *$0* in estate taxes. Considering that it takes little extra time and money to incorporate such a trust into your living trust, it simply makes no sense not to have a bypass trust if your estate is large.

THE MECHANICS OF HOW A BYPASS TRUST WORKS. What makes a bypass trust work is the tax law that allows anyone to pass $600,000 tax-free. This is called an exemption. A bypass trust protects that $600,000 exemption. If the exemption is not used, then the estate is taxed at a *starting* rate of 37 percent, and goes up to 55 percent for estates over $3 million.

This sort of joint living trust is like any other living trust, except that it includes two subtrusts—often called trust A (usually the wife's trust) and trust B (usually the husband's trust.)

John and Julia had three children and an estate worth $1 million. Avoiding probate and reducing estate taxes were their main priorities when planning their estate. They had a joint living trust drawn up which they named "John and Julia's Trust." Their trust incorporated A and B subtrusts. To avoid confusion, they named Julia's subtrust "Julia's Trust" and John's subtrust "John's Trust."

During their life, John and Julia would use their property however they wished, just as anyone with a living trust would. Upon the death of the first spouse, say, John, the two subtrusts would irrevocably come into effect—half the estate ($500,000) would go into John's Trust, and half ($500,000) would go into Julia's Trust. Since John's estate is under the critical $600,000 figure, no estate taxes would be due.

But that's not all. John's Trust would name Julia as the primary beneficiary, and his children as the alternate beneficiaries.

It would also name Julia as the trustee. As a result, Julia would have her own living trust ("Julia's Trust" ) with $500,000 in it, and would also be the trustee and beneficiary of the other $500,000 trust—John's trust.

Not only are no taxes paid on John's estate, but the bypass trust created by John and Julia would avoid all estate taxes when Julia dies too. It is important to remember that a trust is a separate legal entity, and therefore it is the trust, and not Julia, who actually owns the property left in John's Trust. Because Julia never owned the property left in John's Trust, when she dies, her estate is worth $500,000 and not $1 million (as it would be if no bypass trust were created). Since her estate is valued at less than $600,000, no estate taxes would be due.

Had they not established a bypass trust, Julia would have inherited John's $500,000 outright. At Julia's death she would have owned $1 million. John and Julia's children would then have been taxed on the $400,000 they inherited above the $600,000 limit—approximately $70,000 in taxes would have been due. Since many estates have a lot of the assets tied up in real estate, this $70,000 tax would have used up valuable liquid capital. By creating a bypass, or A-B, subtrust, John and Julia were able to give their children an extra $70,000.

After Julia dies, the two subtrusts would then combine again. If the children were adults, the successor trustee could distribute the assets among the kids. If the children were minors, special provisions in the trust would enable the trustee to continue to help them. (See Chapter 20, "Children's Trusts.")

It should be clear that bypass trusts can save taxes only on estates with values of up to $1.2 million, since each spouse is allowed to protect only $600,000. Estates worth more than that will end up paying estate taxes, although a Qualified Terminable Interest Trust (a **QTIP Trust**) can reduce those taxes. (See Chapter 21, "Other Types of Subtrusts.")

RESTRICTIONS ON A BYPASS TRUST. Like any beneficiary of an A-B trust, while she is alive, Julia can use the assets in Julia's

Trust however she wants. Her rights to use the assets in John's Trust (the B trust) are a bit more limited, though. She can use all of the *income* generated by the trust, but very little of the *principal*. The rule to remember is this: her right to use the trust principal is limited to health care, education, support, and maintenance according to her established lifestyle. Aside from the use of principal for health and education, what the IRS also allows is for a beneficiary like Julia to use up to $5,000 or 5 percent per year, whichever is greater, of the trust principal for any reason, not just health and education. Any use beyond that would result in the IRS determining that the beneficiary is in fact the owner of the assets. In that case, the IRS would assess a retroactive estate tax.

Because of this rule, it is possible for the principal of a bypass trust to be depleted over time. This may not be desirable for couples in a second marriage who often want to preserve the principal for their children. In that case, the trust document can restrict or completely prohibit the spouse from dipping into any principal. (See Chapter 21, "Other Types of Subtrusts.")

**The Important Legal Concept to Remember: For a combined estate worth less than $1.2 million, a well-drafted bypass trust can avoid probate and completely eliminate estate taxes. A marital trust can usually work just fine for smaller estates.**

# 20

# SUBTRUSTS II: CHILDREN'S TRUSTS

*Creating an estate for your children*
*Family pot trusts*
*Individual trusts*
*Providing for a child with special needs*

CREATING AN ESTATE FOR YOUR CHILDREN. Before you can leave substantial sums of money to care for your children, you must first have substantial sums of money. Creating an estate is the obvious first step to leaving an estate.

Of course, hard work and good investments are one way to create an estate. But there is an easier way insofar as estate planning is concerned. Estate-planning professionals such as attorneys, financial advisers, and investment counselors have long advocated term life insurance as the easiest way to create an estate worth planning for and leaving.

Term life insurance is a bargain, and nothing is better for ensuring that your children are taken care of after you are gone. A $500,000 term life insurance policy costs about $50 per month. The important thing to understand about term life insurance is that the policy is in effect only for as long as payments are made. If you let the policy lapse, and die subsequently, no proceeds are paid. But if you die while the policy is in effect, the insurance company will pay your beneficiaries the $500,000.

Minors cannot legally own any large sums of money. The way to care for your minor children, then, is to create a children's subtrust and name it as the beneficiary of the policy. You thereby can legally leave enough money for your kids, and your trustee will have the resources to care for your children in accordance with the terms of your trust.

Life insurance proceeds are included as part of your taxable estate. If you plan to leave enough insurance money for your children so that your estate will climb over $600,000, and therefore be subject to estate taxes, you are advised either to create a separate trust to hold ownership of the policy (called an ILIT, see next chapter) or to give ownership of the policy to someone you trust. (For more information on the use of life insurance in estate planning, see Chapter 27, "Life Insurance.")

FAMILY POT TRUSTS. Family pot trusts are usually the preferable estate-planning method when one has minor children. With this type of trust you leave assets for all children in one trust— called a family pot trust—as opposed to creating a separate trust for each individual child. The trustee then uses the family pot trust assets to care for each individual child as needed.

The reason why it is wiser to create one family pot trust instead of individual trusts is that individual trusts mean that your estate is divided equally at your death according to the number of children you have. If you have three kids, each would get an individual trust consisting of one third of your assets. Although this seems to make sense, upon closer examination, this arithmetic approach does not really serve children all that well.

Norman had two children when he made his living trust, aged twelve and two. Wanting to be fair to both children, he set up two separate but equal subtrusts for his kids, effective upon his death. In the intervening ten years before he died, Norman's younger child was diagnosed with a severe learning disability, requiring expensive help. Nevertheless, when Nor-

man died ten years later, his estate was divided equally
between his needy twelve-year-old and his healthy twenty-
two-year-old, who by that time was making a fine living.

While you may love all your children equally, their needs
may be unequal. A family pot trust avoids this dilemma by
allowing the trustee to utilize the money as needed—dispro-
portionately if necessary, equally if not. The trustee is given
instructions to use the money to care for the children as necessary until the youngest child reaches a specified age or upon
the occurrence of a specified event: graduation from college or
marriage, for example. After that, whatever money is left is
either split up evenly or put into separate trusts for each adult
child. (If you have a child who is physically or mentally hand-
icapped, a "special needs" trust should be created specifically
for him or her. See next chapter.)

A family pot trust makes sense because it most closely
resembles how a parent might run things if he remained alive.
Parents spend their money as necessary for each child. If one
needs extra help, she gets it. If not, parents usually try to be fair
and even with all their children. That is just what a family pot
trust says and does.

When creating a family pot trust, it is essential that the
trustee be given broad powers and detailed instructions in your
living trust. This will allow the trustee to use the trust funds
based on her discretion and your stated desires. Your trustee
may or may not be the same person as the guardian. If not,
also make sure to give your trustee the power to assist the
guardian. After all, the guardian is the person who will be raising your children if this all unfortunately comes to pass, and
she will need all the help she can get.

The stated main purpose of the family pot trust should be
to care for the health, education, and welfare of all of your children no matter what age. However, it should not be so one-
sided so as to forbid an adult child from other, less "essential"
things like buying a car or home or starting a business. As long

as these things do not interfere with the main purpose of the trust, instructions should also be given that will enable the trustee to give money to an older child for these needs as well.

INDIVIDUAL TRUSTS. Separate individual trusts come into play at two times: either upon the conclusion of the family pot trust, or instead of a family pot trust if all children are already adults.

Although individual trusts may make a lot of sense for adult children since they enable the children to know exactly how much money they have, they can also create resentment. Not many adults like being told how to handle money. Creating an individual trust for an adult child may imply that you do not trust the child's judgment. Whether to create an individual trust depends upon the amount of money and the maturity of the child. More money or less maturity increases the need for a trust.

Like any other type of trust, an individual children's trust must name a trustee and a beneficiary. Even if you have four children and thus, subsequently, four separate individual trusts, you can still name one person to be the trustee for each trust. Being a trustee is a big job, and it should not be given to someone who is irresponsible or whom your children do not get along with.

Each child's trust should tell the trustee to use the money for the health, education, maintenance, and support of the child. It is a good idea to instruct the trustee to be liberal and generous with the money since he or she will be dealing with adults who can make their own decisions.

Such trusts are usually drafted to allow for mandatory distributions of trust principal at specific times. While you can certainly leave an entire inheritance for a child at a specific age, say, twenty-five, it usually makes more sense to spread the money out in intervals. This enables a child to have more than one chance at using the money wisely. The decisions a twenty-five-year-old would make with $50,000 may be quite different from those she would make at thirty-five.

The possibilities for ultimate distribution are quite varied. Some options are

- *At various ages:* Many people like the idea of leaving one-third every five years for ten years—twenty-five, thirty, and thirty-five are common.
- *Upon the occurrence of various events:* This option ties an event to an age—"Upon graduation from college or the age of twenty-two, whichever comes first"; "Upon marriage or the age of thirty, whichever comes first"; "When buying a house or the age of thirty-five, whichever comes first."
- *Whenever the child requests the money:* A daughter who has proven herself to be financially responsible can be given permission to request and get whatever amounts she wants whenever she wants.
- *No mandatory distribution:* If you have a child who has a gambling problem, who drinks too much, who is a spendthrift, etc., you may not want mandatory distributions. Instead, the money can remain in trust and the trustee can allocate the money as she sees fit. Another option for a troublesome heir is a subtrust called a **spendthrift trust.** The unique characteristic of a spendthrift trust is that it usually allocates only income, but not principal, to the beneficiary; the principal is retained for a different ultimate beneficiary.
- *Other:* You can be as creative as you wish. For instance, you might want to keep half of an inheritance in trust for a child until he reaches the age of fifty-five, so that the money can be used for his retirement.

You should also consider what you want done with separate children's trust funds should a child die before all distributions are complete. There are two options. Either you can leave it up to your child to distribute her coming inheritance in accordance with her own will or trust, or you yourself can direct where the remaining money due should go. Remember, it is only the money *left to be distributed* that you can control. Money already distributed to children is theirs to do with, and give away, as they wish.

PROVIDING FOR A CHILD WITH SPECIAL NEEDS. Planning for a child or grandchild with a physical or mental disability is not easy. Not only must the trustee be selected with much scrutiny but so too must the special needs trust be crafted with much care.

The problem is that if the trust is not drawn up correctly, the special needs beneficiary could lose valuable and needed assistance—things like Social Security income, medical assistance, educational grants, and the like. Since such benefits usually depend upon the financial needs of the recipient, a disabled beneficiary improperly left a lot of money could lose his eligibility for such assistance. Now, if you can afford to leave enough money for *all possible needs* of the special needs heir, you obviously do not need to worry about creating a trust that protects possible government assistance. This is not the case for most people. The key, then, is to have a trust drafted that helps your loved one while still allowing him to retain his eligibility.

The trust created would be like any other individual children's trust, except that it should have the following provisions:

- *The trust should last for the entire life of the child:* Since such children cannot care for themselves easily, the trust should last the entire life of the child, and appropriate trustee arrangements and designations must be made.

- *All possible power must be given to the trustee:* Under Social Security Administration rules, the trust will not count against the beneficiary if he or she has no right to draw from the trust. Therefore, all discretionary power to distribute the trust principal and income must be given to the trustee.

- *The beneficiary can have no right to revoke the trust:* Beneficiaries usually have the right to go to court, end a trust, and use the assets however they wish. A special needs trust must forbid this.

These are just general rules. This area of the law is state-specific and subject to much change and interpretation. Find an attorney knowledgeable about this complex area of law.

**The Important Legal Concept to Remember: Leaving money for a child in a way that best serves his or her interest takes a lot of forethought. Family pot trusts are best for minors; individual trusts with periodic distributions are often best for adults. Special needs trusts must be drafted by an expert.**

# 21

# SUBTRUSTS III: OTHER TYPES OF SUBTRUSTS

*Tax-savings trusts*
*Trusts for second marriages*
*How to give to charity*

Aside from bypass trusts, family pot trusts, individual children's trusts, and special needs trusts, there are many other subtrusts that can be tailored to meet different situations. Some of the most common are listed below.

TAX-SAVINGS TRUSTS. Aside from bypass trusts, there are other kinds of subtrusts that also save estate taxes, depending upon the circumstances.

A QTIP trust is a trust that allows the estate to delay paying any taxes until the second death, no matter how much money is in the estate. Remember that bypass trusts save on estate taxes only for estates up to $1.2 million. Anything over that amount is taxed at the time of the first death. QTIP trusts avoid this.

> Mike and Ethel have an estate worth $2.5 million. Their living trust created three separate subtrusts—"Mike's Trust," "Ethel's Trust," and the "QTIP Trust." The sum of $600,000 went into each bypass trust, and $1.3 million went into the QTIP. Mike died ten years before Ethel.

Under normal circumstances, without a QTIP trust, Mike's estate would owe estate taxes within nine months of his death on the $1.3 million over the $1.2 million bypass trust limit. The first advantage of a QTIP is that no taxes would be due for ten years, until the death of Ethel.

The second advantage is that the QTIP can be drawn up in such a way that it would allow the surviving spouse to use not only the income from the QTIP but the *principal* as well. This is a great benefit. It allows the surviving spouse to use as much of the QTIP trust money as she sees fit. A surviving spouse could actually use up *the entire amount left in the QTIP*. In the case of Mike and Ethel, Ethel could spend the $1.3 in the QTIP. Since taxes are not due on that money until her death, no estate tax whatsoever would be paid on their $2.5 million estate. QTIPs, like special needs trusts, call for advanced estate planning, and an estate-planning specialist must be retained.

An ILIT (irrevocable life insurance trust) is another way to save large amounts on estate taxes. Because proceeds from life insurance are included as part of your taxable estate, any substantial amount of money received from life insurance can push your estate past $600,000. Because an ILIT owns your policy, when you die, it is the ILIT, and not your estate, that the policy is counted against. And since your life insurance proceeds are, then, not part of your taxable estate, estate taxes on the proceeds of the policy are avoided. Another option with life insurance proceeds, other than an ILIT, is to give ownership of the policy to someone else.

Finally, a GST (**generation skipping trust**) is a type of tax-savings trust used by wealthy grandparents to care for their children and grandchildren. The GST allows such people to transfer up to $1 million tax-free. In order to use a GST, the money must be put in trust for the children of the grantor, and only the income generated by the trust can be used by that generation. When that generation dies (i.e., the grantor's children), up to $1 million in trust principal can be transferred to the next generation (the grandchildren) tax-free.

TRUSTS FOR SECOND MARRIAGES. Spouses in second marriages usually have two estate-planning goals in mind. They want to care for their new spouse, yet they still desire to retain as much of their assets as possible, ultimately for their children. This conundrum is fairly easily resolved by using a trust without an acronym—a property control trust.

A property control trust is just another type of subtrust of your living trust, and is not unlike a bypass trust. Trust assets are kept for use by the new spouse during her life, but limits are placed on her ability to dip into trust principal. For example, a home owned by a husband can be placed in trust for his surviving wife for her lifetime. While she is alive, she is allowed to live in the house, yet she is prohibited from selling it or taking out a loan against it. Upon her death or remarriage, the house will go to the husband's children.

The limits that can be placed on this type of trust are numerous. The surviving spouse can be given the right to use the property or can be given income generated from the property. A surviving child can be made trustee. Upon remarriage, all rights to trust property can be terminated.

HOW TO GIVE TO CHARITY. If you have an estate under $600,000, you can simply name a charity as a beneficiary of your living trust, and allocate an amount to be received. Larger estates, in order to save on possible estate taxes, should create a subtrust—preferably a charitable remainder trust, but possibly a **charitable lead trust**.

A charitable remainder trust requires a large piece of income-producing property, like real estate or stock, to work. The charity gets use of the property, but the income generated by the asset is used by the trust maker during his lifetime. Upon the death of the trust maker, the asset in its entirety is transferred to the charity. The charity is usually named trustee.

There are several benefits to this arrangement. Because the trust maker has transferred a large asset into trust for an ultimate beneficiary aside from himself, the asset is excluded from his estate for the purpose of calculating estate taxes. Yet since the property generates income for the trust maker during his life, he continues to get benefits from the asset. Also, the placing in trust of an asset that probably has greatly increased in value during his life enables the trust maker to avoid possible capital gains taxes.

A charitable lead trust works in the exact opposite manner. With this type of trust, the charity receives the income from the property for a set number of years. When the period is over, the asset reverts back to the estate and is given to whomever the owner chooses to receive it. A charitable lead trust makes sense for a couple who can comfortably live without the income of such an asset during their life. Charitable lead trusts are not highly recommended as the grantor is responsible for all income taxes generated by the trust, even though the income goes to the charity.

There are several important restrictions on both types of charitable trusts. First, they can come into effect only while you are alive, not upon your death, as with most subtrusts. Also, they are *irrevocable*. Once you create and fund a charitable trust, you cannot later terminate the trust and get your property back, as you can with a living trust. Finally, to get desired tax savings, you must name a tax-exempt charity as the beneficiary, known as a 501(c)(3) entity, to the IRS.

**The Important Legal Concept to Remember: Depending upon your estate-planning goals, there is a trust to suit your needs.**

# 22

# NAMING A TRUSTEE

*What a trustee does*

*Naming a trustee*

*How to make your trustee's life easier*

WHAT A TRUSTEE DOES. You actually need to pick two trustees: one to act as trustee during your life, and the second to act as trustee after your death. While you are alive, you should be the trustee of your living trust. You will need to name a **successor trustee** to administer your estate after you pass away. This basically entails distributing your property in accordance with your wishes. It should be a fairly quick and simple job in that case.

If, however, you are going to have some ongoing subtrusts as part of your living trust, then the successor trustee's duties become far more complex. Ongoing subtrusts usually last for many years, and your chosen trustee will likely be involved in many financial arrangements on behalf of the beneficiaries and trust. Specifically, your trustee will have the following responsibilities:

1. *To administer the trust:* Your trustee's first and foremost responsibility is to follow the terms of the trust as you set forth, distribute the money pursuant to your instructions, and make sure that your goals, desires, and commitments are carried out. This also means filing appropriate taxes and dealing with any other administrative duties.

2. *To invest your money:* **The prudent investor rule** is a legal axiom that dictates that a trustee has a legal duty to use the funds entrusted to him wisely and invest it responsibly. Whether or not there is a lot of money involved, you will need someone responsible, knowledgeable, savvy, and moral.

3. *To be a* **fiduciary***:* A fiduciary duty is the highest duty imposed by law. Trustees are fiduciaries. They have a legal obligation to deal with the trust and beneficiaries with the utmost good faith and honesty.

4. *To deal with your loved ones:* This actually may be the most taxing and important duty your trustee will have. Your trustee will be intimately involved with the finances of your loved ones. Some trustees become surrogate parents to the beneficiaries. Because of this close interaction, your trustee should be empathetic yet objective, caring yet strong. It is not an easy balance.

These often difficult, sometimes mutually exclusive, roles make the job of trustee a very hard one. It is an extremely responsible and demanding job requiring discretion, compassion, and wisdom. Because so much money, so many dreams, and so much personal intimacy will be involved in the running of your trust, the choice of trustee is among the most important you will make in this process.

NAMING A TRUSTEE. The trust maker is almost always the trustee during her life. Your duties while running your trust during your life are minimal. It really is only a matter of making sure that your property is properly transferred into the name of the trust (see next chapter).

It is often a good idea to name a **cotrustee** along with yourself. The reason for naming a cotrustee is so that there will be someone who will be empowered to run your trust should you become disabled. Having a cotrustee avoids any lag time insofar as the running of the trust goes during an incapacity. Married couples should obviously pick each other. Single people usually name a sibling or adult child. Your cotrustee does not even need to do anything while you are alive; you can run the trust without her. And if you are unhappy with your cotrustee, you can dismiss her at any time. Remember, your trust is your own personal fiefdom and you can do as you please.

The real question comes when it is time to name a trustee for your ongoing subtrusts. The term is not called "trustee" for nothing; you must implicitly trust this person. When naming a trustee or cotrustees for your ongoing subtrusts, you can either name an institution, like a bank, or you can name an individual.

Banks, private trust companies, and other financial institutions are well versed in the running of trusts. They have the personnel and expertise to do a professional job, and have the financial know-how to make good investments. Another advantage of having an institutional trustee is that it can afford to pay for any mistakes made in administering the trust, whereas many individuals cannot.

When he died, Ted had an estate worth $250,000, and a life insurance policy naming his living trust as beneficiary worth another $250,000. Ted named his best friend, Sal, to be the trustee of the children's trust since Sal was a financial adviser. Sal invested the money wisely for several years, but then ran into some personal financial problems. Although he tried not to, Sal succumbed to the pressure, and secretly borrowed $250,000 from the trust. The bailout failed to work, Sal declared bankruptcy, and he lost half of the trust principal intended for Ted's children.

While no bank would ever get into this type of dilemma, mistakes are made and money is lost, however well intentioned the trustee. Institutional trustees have the financial ability (and insurance protection) to compensate any beneficiary for such a loss.

Despite these advantages, choosing an institutional trustee is *not highly recommended.* The main problem is that a living trust is a document borne of love. No institution can administer it with the same degree of compassion and personal knowledge that a trusted friend or relative could. Banks are simply too impersonal. Employees quit or get fired. People come and go. No bank would care about your son as your brother would.

That is why the second choice—a trusted and knowledgeable individual—is the better way to go when choosing a trustee for an ongoing subtrust. If, for example, you plan on having a children's family pot trust, you stand a far better chance of providing your children with the love and guidance you would want for them if you chose someone who knows and loves your children.

This desired compassion is a potential drawback. Because this person *will* know your family so well, he or she will not be nearly as objective as an institution might be. Your trust should ideally be drafted to allow your trustee great discretion when helping the beneficiaries. You must be sure that your choice will act fairly, will not have preconceived prejudices toward a beneficiary, and will do her best to carry out your wishes, even if those wishes may sometimes conflict with her own judgment.

One way to avoid this problem is to name cotrustees so that two opinions are heard, or even three trustees with a majority vote required to make decisions. This will ensure that a fairly objective standard will be used when making decisions. It will also surely be cumbersome.

Finally, because your subtrusts will be continuing for some time, you will also need to name an alternate trustee should your chosen trustee or trustees resign or die. And since the job is usually fairly complicated, again, make sure to get the alternate's approval *before* naming him.

HOW TO MAKE YOUR TRUSTEE'S LIFE EASIER. Anything you can do now to make your trustee's life easier later will be much appreciated. Here are four things you can do:

1. *Have a long chat with your trustee:* Sit down with your trustee now, before it's too late, go over your trust with him, and make sure he understands what it is you want.

2. *Have your trust drafted in plain English:* Many living trusts are drafted in "boilerplate" legal language. Clauses like "the trustee shall be given all authority under the laws of this state to care for the beneficiary" abound. What does that really tell your trustee? Nothing. It will likely cost more, but make sure that your attorney drafts your trust in plain English. That way, your trustee will know what you want and will be able to refer to the trust document to ascertain your intentions easily.

3. *Be thorough:* There are no limits as to what you can say in your trust. Be sure that you include detailed explanations and instructions for your trustee. The less she has to guess what you would have wanted, the better for everybody concerned.

4. *Pay your trustee:* Your trust should have a provision that will provide your trustee with money for the time and energy expended. This will be much appreciated, despite protestations to the contrary.

**The Important Legal Concept to Remember: Few choices you make in your life will have more long-term ramifications than who you decide should be the trustee of your ongoing subtrust. Pick someone whose judgment you inherently believe in, and who can deal well with your loved ones.**

# 23

# FUNDING YOUR LIVING TRUST

The importance of funding your trust

Funding your trust

How to get assets you missed into your trust

THE IMPORTANCE OF FUNDING YOUR TRUST. So you finally did it. You went to an attorney, had a living trust drawn up with all the bells and whistles, subtrusts and beneficiary designations, and you brought it home. You put it away, thought you covered all possible bases, and then you died. Despite all your planning and good intentions, your entire estate will go through probate, and not a penny in estate taxes will have been saved.

Why? Because you failed to do the last necessary thing—you failed to fund your living trust by transferring your assets into it. If you fail to fund your living trust, your trust is nothing more than a *worthless piece of paper.*

Any property you own that is not made part of your trust will go through probate. That is why it is absolutely necessary to put everything you own into the trust. Remember that a trust is nothing more than a container for your property. Just as a container without contents is useless, so too is a trust without assets.

FUNDING YOUR TRUST. How assets are deposited into the trust depends upon what kind of assets they are. You may need the help of an attorney, stockbroker, life insurance agent, and/or accountant when transferring the following properties:

- *Real estate:* Title to your home, land, vacation cabin, or other real estate must be transferred to the name of the trust by using a **deed**. You need to deed over the property to the new owner—your living trust. It must then be recorded at the county recorder's office.

  For example, Phil and Mindy would sign a deed that states something like "Grantor (owner) Phil and Mindy Sobel hereby grants the following property to Phil and Mindy Sobel, Trustees or Successors of the Sobel Family Trust, dated 9/27/95." The deed would describe the land transferred. After the deed was recorded, the trust would own the property. Thereafter, Phil and Mindy would continue to use their home as before, with the only difference being that their trust, which they are the trustees of, would own their home. There would be no tax consequences or changes with their loan because of this transfer. *Make sure to get an attorney to do this.*

- *Financial accounts:* Stocks, bonds, mutual funds, money market accounts, and other investment accounts also need to be transferred into the name of the trust. Ask your broker to do this for you, or pay the necessary fee if you have no broker. Your broker will need the original certificates to make these changes.

  Checking and savings accounts, CDs, IRAs, and other bank accounts should also be changed. *You will not need to get new checks.* All you need to do is change the signature card; your checks can continue to bear the name presently on the checks. Your bank may require proof that your trust in fact exists. Have your attorney draft a "certification" for this purpose.

· *Life insurance, retirement accounts, annuities, etc.*: Assets with beneficiary designations such as these must name a new beneficiary—your living trust. Life insurance designation alterations can be accomplished quickly by your agent. Retirement plans may require a "spousal consent" form signed by your mate in order to alter the named beneficiary. Check with the administrator of the plan.

· *Businesses:* If your business is a sole proprietorship or partnership, you will need to **assign** your share of the assets to your trust. Your lawyer can draw up the appropriate assignment. If your business is a corporation, your company's corporate secretary will need to issue new stock certificates to you as trustee for your trust.

· *Personal property:* You should also have all personal property—things such as furniture, china, televisions, and such—assigned to the trust as well. Do not transfer your autos to the trust as it is usually not needed, and it may cause complications with registration and insurance. (Although if your car is an expensive investment-type car, then it should be made part of your trust.) Since most states require assets in excess of around sixty thousand dollars to even open probate (called the small-estate exception), a regular car will not go through probate. Just have your living trust state where you want the car to go. However, each state's laws differ in this regard, and an attorney must be consulted as to the amount of the small-estate exception for your state.

HOW TO GET ASSETS YOU MISSED INTO YOUR TRUST. It is unlikely that everything you own at the time of your death will have been transferred to your trust. Some people fail to make the so-called extra effort to transfer all assets initially, although an attorney can simply be paid to do this. Others forget to transfer assets bought *after* the trust is created and funded. There are a couple of ways to get those forgotten assets into the trust.

The first is a **pour-over will**. A pour-over will simply says, "I leave everything owned by me, not already in my living trust, to my living trust." If the amount left is less than the small-estate exception of your state, then your estate will still bypass probate. If your assets exceed the required small-estate level, probate will occur. *Everyone needs a will, even people with expensive, comprehensive living trusts.*

The second method is a **durable special power of attorney**. A power of attorney is a powerful document you sign that permits someone you name to make legal decisions on your behalf. (A *general* power of attorney basically enables the person given this power to do almost anything in your name. It is often a *bad* idea to give someone a general power of attorney.) What you want is a *special* power of attorney. It has one function: to permit your designated person, called your "attorney-in-fact," to transfer your property into your trust. It is used most often when someone falls ill and cannot do this for himself. By giving a special power of attorney to your lawyer and/or other trusted individual, you ensure that whatever was left out of the trust will make its way there before it is too late.

**The Important Legal Concept to Remember: Getting a living trust is a two-step process. Not only must you create the trust but you *must* also fund the trust. Failing to transfer your assets makes the trust worthless in more ways than one.**

# OTHER ESTATE-PLANNING OPTIONS

# 24

# GIFTS

*What is a gift?*
*Using gifts to reduce your estate and avoid taxes*
*Gifts of property that is appreciating*
*How to give a house to your kids and still avoid taxes*
*Gifts to minors*
*Gifts to charity*

Planning to give a **gift** of your property while you are *alive* is often a smart estate-planning option. Many people feel that they would rather share their estate with their loved ones while they are still around than after they are gone; they get to share in the joy while also knowing that they made life easier for those they love.

That giving a gift during one's life can be a joyous event is reason enough to consider this estate-planning option. That there are significant tax and estate-planning benefits too can often make this option a fine choice indeed. This is especially true if your estate is worth more than $600,000 or your combined estate with your mate is worth more than $1.2 million.

WHAT IS A GIFT? While what constitutes a gift may seem self-evident to you, it may not surprise you that it is not so to the IRS. Legally, a gift is a gratuitous voluntary transfer of property to another person. Gifts can include the obvious (personal property, real estate, cash) and the obscure (interest-free loans [the free interest is the gift], forgiving a debt, life insurance).

To the IRS, two factors are important in determining whether a gift has been made. First is the **donor's** intent. Is this really a gift or does it merely look like a gift? There must be a true intent to release the property to another. If there is doubt, Uncle Sam often looks to the second factor to determine the donor's intent: delivery, and acceptance by the recipient. The person to whom the gift is made must receive and exert control over the property. The donor can no longer hold power over the property for a gift to be deemed valid. If the donor retains control, the IRS will conclude that there was no intent to make a gift.

For example, if you give your son your Microsoft stock certificates, but you continue to receive the dividends, there has been no gift. Similarly, if you deed over an apartment house to your children, but continue to receive the rent, no gift has been made for estate-planning purposes. Since one of the major estate-planning benefits of giving a gift is the chance to avoid taxes legally, it is important to make sure that complete control of the property is relinquished.

USING GIFTS TO REDUCE YOUR ESTATE AND AVOID TAXES. Indeed, one of the main benefits of gift giving as an estate-planning tool is the ability to transfer property free of federal taxes. As explained previously, this is important only if your taxable estate exceeds $600,000 individually, or $1.2 million combined with a spouse's.

In order to pass gifts tax-free, planning is necessary. A one-time gift of $600,000 would not do. The rule to remember is this: *Any one person can give away up to $10,000 a year to any one individual without paying federal gift or estate taxes. A couple can give away $20,000 a year per recipient tax-free.* This is called the annual gift exemption. If Aaron and Jillian had three children, they could legally give each child $20,000 a year, for a grand total of $60,000 per year, without paying any tax. Of course, they could give more, but anything more than $20,000 is taxed starting at 37 percent. In order to give their children the $600,000, then, Aaron and Jillian would need to give their children $60,000 a year for ten years. Planning is necessary.

It is also important to understand that gifts *under* $10,000 have no effect on the $600,000 amount that can pass tax-free at death. A gift of $10,000 or under still allows you to pass $600,000 tax-free at your death. That is not true for gifts *over* $10,000. Gifts over $10,000 *reduce the amount that can be given away tax-free* at death. If Aaron and Jillian gave that "extra" $600,000 to one child in one year instead of to three kids over ten years, they would be $580,000 over the annual tax-free gift-giving limit since they can give away only $20,000 a year tax-free to any individual. The amount they could pass at death would correspondingly be reduced by $580,000. Instead of being able to pass $1.2 million free of federal estate taxes, the $600,000 gift would have reduced the amount they could pass tax-free to $620,000.

GIFTS OF PROPERTY THAT IS APPRECIATING. If you are concerned that your estate will surpass the $600,000 limit upon your death, you may want to consider reducing your taxable estate by giving away property that is likely to appreciate significantly—real estate, stock, businesses.

When he made his will, Simon figured that his estate was probably worth around $600,000, and therefore he did not need to make any gifts during his lifetime. One of his favorite assets was a computer stock that he bought during an initial public offering. Although the stock was worth $20,000 when he made his will, the company hit it big soon thereafter, and the stock jumped in value by the time Simon died. His estate was valued at $700,000. The last $100,000 was heavily taxed.

Had Simon given this asset to his son before he died, he would have paid taxes only on the $10,000 that was over the

$10,000 tax-free gift limit. Instead, his son paid taxes on $100,000. A lifetime gift of an appreciable asset can avoid substantial estate taxes.

HOW TO GIVE A HOUSE TO YOUR KIDS AND STILL AVOID TAXES. Many parents want to give a house, or the money to buy a house, to their children. House giving has these estate-planning benefits:

- Giving the gift of a home reduces the size of a taxable estate when necessary.
- Even if your estate does not come close to the magical $600,000 figure, if you are older, giving your children your home may help you qualify for Medicaid. And since Medicaid often places liens on homes, removing your house from your estate will ensure that it will be your kids, not the government, who gets the family home. Because Medicaid liens are retroactive some thirty months from the date of delivery of the medical care, if you anticipate that you may use Medicaid, plan ahead.

One potential problem when giving a gift of a house to a married child is that daughters- or sons-in-law may claim an interest in the house if your child divorces or dies. Although gifts to a married child are legally considered the separate asset of that child, be safe. *Make sure to have a written agreement signed by all parties concerned that the house is a "separate asset" of your child and is not to be considered a marital asset.*

If you do want to give a child a house, or its equivalent, here are two ways to do so and still avoid the $10,000 gift-tax limit:

1. Buy the house yourself, then sell it to your kids for a reasonable price, and take a 100 percent mortgage. Structure the deal so that the annual mortgage payments are no more than $10,000. Forgive the annual payments, and presto: no

taxes are due. Obviously, if you can afford to do this, you can afford a 100 percent mortgage, and your children need not pay a penny out of pocket for the house.

2. Similarly, you can simply lend your children the money for the house at an interest rate that pays no more than $10,000 per year. Afterward, forgive the loan payments each year, and again no tax is due.

If you choose to do either one, you are strongly advised to seek the assistance of an attorney so that all possible problems, with the IRS and otherwise, are avoided.

GIFTS TO MINORS. Giving a gift to a child or grandchild is really less about reducing the size of your estate and more about protecting your young children or grandchildren.

Children cannot legally own property and cannot make enforceable decisions about what to do with property. Instead, two laws have been enacted by most states which authorize the creation of custodial trust accounts for minors: the Uniform Gifts to Minors Act (UGMA), and the Uniform Transfer to Minors Act (UTMA).

These two laws allow you to open up trust accounts in the names of the minor children, retain control of the property by naming yourself or your spouse as custodian, and then transfer money into the accounts. The money transferred into a child's trust account is **irrevocable**—you cannot later withdraw it. As custodian, you are in charge of the account. It becomes the child's unrestricted property usually at the age of twenty-one, although it depends upon the state. UGMA and UTMA trust accounts can be opened at banks, savings and loans, and stock brokerage houses.

The tax considerations for such accounts are few. As with other gifts, gifts over $10,000 to a child's trust account are a taxable event. After the age of thirteen, the income generated by these accounts becomes taxable income to the child, and a so-called "kiddie tax" is levied by the IRS. The rate is far less than you pay. You also need to name a successor custodian for the account in the event of your death. If you do not, all funds in the account will revert back to your estate and will be taxed accordingly should you die before the child reaches the age of eighteen.

GIFTS TO CHARITY. The estate-planning benefits of giving to a charity are twofold. First, all gifts made to charities are exempt from the $10,000 federal gift-tax limit—you can give *any amount* desired to a charity tax-free. Second, because of this, gifts to charities can greatly reduce your taxable estate when needed.

Not all charities need apply, though; only charities that are determined to be nonprofit under IRS code 501(c)(3) are exempt from taxes. Gifts to other charities will be taxed at the standard gift-tax rate. If you want to give away a substantial asset but still want to retain the income off the property during your life, you need to set up a charitable remainder trust. (See Chapter 21, "Other Types of Subtrusts.")

**The Important Legal Concept to Remember: Gifts benefit both the recipient and the donor when made during the donor's life. A gift can help reduce the size of a large taxable estate, and can provide needed assistance to a younger generation.**

# JOINT TENANCY

Estate planning is not an easy thing; decisions must be well thought out and carefully enacted. For many, it is too much work. A traditional tool used by people to simplify the estate-planning process has been to own property as "joint tenants with a right of survivorship." When one joint tenant dies, the other owns the entire property outright by operation of law. It is sometimes, but not usually, a good idea. ("Tenancy by the entirety" is the same as joint tenancy except that it is reserved for married couples. All issues discussed herein apply equally to tenancy by the entirety.)

JOINT TENANCY. Joint tenancy is a way for two or more persons, called joint tenants, to own property. Cars, boats, planes, and bank accounts are all often held in joint tenancy, but most often joint tenancy is associated with ownership of real estate. The distinguishing feature of joint tenancy is that should one joint tenant die, the property *automatically* transfers to the other joint tenant(s) by operation of law. As such, probate is avoided.

Brian and Sarah did not want to spend a lot of money and time on their estate plan. Since their house was their major asset, they transferred title to themselves as joint tenants. When Brian died, the house transferred to Sarah automatically, and there was nothing to probate.

Because of this unique characteristic, this "right of survivorship," joint tenancy has been called the "poor man's will." It is not hard to understand why. If your major asset is your home, as is the case for many people, you can simultaneously avoid probate and protect your spouse by simply putting title to your house in joint tenancy. Not only is probate avoided but so too are complex estate plans and costly lawyers.

Joint tenancy is different from the other prevalent method of real estate ownership—"tenancy in common." A tenant in common owns an undivided share of the property. For example, three joint tenants may own a rental unit, and each would thereby own 33 percent of the property. A tenant in common can sell or give away his share. Tenancy in common *does not* allow for the automatic transfer of the property at death that joint tenancy does.

If joint tenancy sounds too good to be true, that is because it is. Joint tenancy is often a false prophet. Alaska, Pennsylvania, Tennessee, and Texas have all but abolished joint tenancy because of problems it may cause.

PROBLEMS WITH JOINT TENANCY. There are many troubling aspects of joint tenancy as an estate-planning alternative. First of all, while it is true that joint tenancy does avoid probate at the death of the first joint tenant, it does not avoid it at the death of the surviving joint tenant. When the second joint tenant dies, the property will go through probate. All joint tenancy really does, then, is delay, not avoid, probate.

If both joint tenants die at the same time, in a car accident, for example, the probate problem doubles. Without a will, and without a joint tenant to transfer the property to, the law mandates that not one but two probates be opened.

If one of the joint tenants becomes incapacitated, other prob-

one who paid less. If a father decides to add his son onto his $100,000 home as a joint tenant in order to avoid probate, the IRS would consider that a $40,000 gift. Here is how that is computed: the father is giving his son half of his house—$50,000—but the first $10,000 is tax-free.

Joint tenancy also does not reduce the size of your taxable estate for federal estate tax purposes. If you are married, then half the value of the property will apply to the size of your estate. If you are not married, then the amount depends upon the percentage of the down payment you put into the property. If you put in 50 percent, that means that 50 percent of the value of the property is part of your estate. If you put the entire amount down, that means that the entire property will apply to your estate for tax purposes.

Even worse, for unmarried joint tenants, the IRS *presumes* that the first joint tenant to die contributed *all of the money* toward the purchase of the property. This means that 100 percent of the value of the property will likely apply to the taxable estate of the first to die for death-tax purposes. If that value pushes the taxable estate over $600,000, then estate taxes will be due. This also means that unless good records are kept, the property will apply to the size of the estate upon the second death as well.

Walter bought a cabin with his sister Mary that they owned for many years. They held title as joint tenants. When Walter died, Mary could not prove that she contributed to the down payment, and therefore the entire value of the house was included in Walter's estate and taxes were paid on it. Thereafter, Mary owned the house outright, and taxes were paid on the entire value of the house for a second time when she died.

WHEN TO USE JOINT TENANCY. Despite all these drawbacks, joint tenancy may be useful in certain, limited situations.

Joint tenancy may make sense for a young married couple

lems arise. Should the healthy joint tenant want to sell or refinance the property, she will have a difficult time doing so since she cannot act without the approval of the incapacitated joint tenant. A conservatorship proceeding in probate court will have to be opened.

One way to avoid this problem is to have a durable special power of attorney drawn up for each joint tenant. A durable special power of attorney for financial matters allows you to name someone to act on your behalf insofar as legal matters are concerned. Since it is a very powerful document that can easily be abused, be *very careful* as to whom you name your "attorney-in-fact." But even then—even if you get a power of attorney—when you go to resell the house, there may still be a problem with escrow or title insurance. If you choose to use joint tenancy, don't say you were not warned.

Another problem with joint tenancy is the possibility of ending up owning the joint tenancy with a stranger. A joint tenancy can be terminated by either party by selling his or her share. The result is that the new owner becomes a tenant in common with the old owner.

> Ellen and her best friend, Shelly, bought a cabin and decided to hold title as joint tenants. After a falling out, Shelly decided to sell her share of the cabin. She sold it to a stranger, who became tenants in common with Ellen.

It is also important to realize that when you die, you cannot leave your share of the joint tenancy property in your will because your share automatically transfers to your joint tenant at your death. You could own a condo with a friend and your spouse will never see a penny from it.

There are potential tax problems to consider. Recall that gifts over $10,000 in any one year require the filing of a gift-tax return and payment of gift taxes. If the joint tenants pay disproportionate amounts for the joint property, the IRS considers the difference paid a gift by the one who paid more to the

since neither is likely to die soon. Should one partner die, the other will own the property, and the likelihood of a second probate would be remote. Here, probate is avoided, as are legal fees.

Married couples whose home is their only significant asset can possibly utilize joint tenancy as an alternative estate plan. Probate will be avoided at the first death, and expensive lawyers will not be needed. If the couple plans to have the surviving spouse create a living trust after the first spouse dies, even better.

If no other estate plan has been made and a death is approaching, transferring property to joint tenancy is a quick and easy will substitute. In such a situation your personal property (cars, furniture, etc.) can also be deemed joint tenancy property by drafting a document to that effect, having it signed by both parties, and having the document notarized. By so doing, you can avoid probate on these assets as well.

**The Important Legal Concept to Remember: Joint tenancy looks better than it actually is. It is usually best to try to avoid it as an estate-planning method.**

# 26

# PAY-ON-DEATH
# ACCOUNTS

Pay-on-death bank accounts
Jointly held safe deposit boxes
Transfer-on-death security accounts
Retirement plans

As can be seen throughout this section, there are a variety of ways to transfer property to your loved ones that are inexpensive and simple, yet still allow you to avoid probate.

Another of these methods is the payable-on-death account, sometimes called a POD account. This is a financial account that allows the owner to name a beneficiary to receive the account upon the death of the owner. All you need to do is open a POD account at the right institution, designate a beneficiary whom you want to receive the account, and upon your death the money *automatically* becomes the property of your beneficiary. Probate is avoided, and the money transfers instantly. Not every state has POD accounts, so you will need to check with a lawyer in your area.

PAY-ON-DEATH BANK ACCOUNTS. These bank accounts are sometimes called **totten trusts**. They operate just as any other POD account. *You* open the account, *you* control the money while you are alive, and *you* designate a beneficiary. Remember, this is a pay-on-*death* account; the beneficiary has no control over the account while you are alive. You can even close the account before you die should you change your mind. Because of its wonderful flexibility, POD bank accounts are a fine probate-avoiding estate-planning tool.

POD accounts are different from joint tenancy bank accounts. The main difference is that the other person on a joint tenancy bank account has equal access and equal right to use the money in the account, whereas the beneficiary of a POD account has no such right.

Opening a POD account is easy. Your bank or financial institution will have a form to fill out naming you as the owner and your designated choice as the beneficiary. Deposit the money and that is that. Upon your death, the money will be considered part of your taxable estate for federal tax purposes, but will not be part of your probate estate.

You cannot use a POD account to disinherit a spouse. Part of each state's probate code mandates that the spouse gets a percentage of the deceased's estate, even if the will leaves that spouse nothing. So, even though you may leave fifty thousand dollars to your lover in a POD account, it does not necessarily mean he or she will get it.

Also, these accounts should not be used to leave money to minor children. Since children cannot legally own property, leaving them money this way is a similar exercise in futility.

JOINTLY HELD SAFE DEPOSIT BOXES. Like other accounts at a bank, a safe deposit box too can be jointly owned, thereby allowing the contents of the box to pass to the co-owner upon the death of either owner.

One problem, though, insofar as estate planning goes, is that many states have laws mandating that safe deposit boxes be sealed at the death of the owner. Since cash is often kept in safe deposit boxes, and since cash is often needed when someone dies, storing money in a safe deposit box may be self-defeating. The person who needs the money often cannot get to it for months after the death. A better option might be to open a POD bank account naming the appropriate party as the beneficiary so that money will be available when it is needed most. It also follows that estate-planning documents such as wills and living trusts should not be stored in a safe deposit box that may be sealed.

TRANSFER ON DEATH SECURITY ACCOUNTS. Some states permit you to use beneficiary designations on your securities accounts, thereby allowing the security to transfer to the person of your choice upon your death. The advantage to this process is the same as with other POD accounts—probate is avoided and money is quickly transferred. The disadvantage is the same too—absent a trustee and a living trust, beneficiary designations can create instant access to a lot of wealth among grieving and/or immature people. Again, if your desire is to have someone oversee the use of a large inheritance, you need a living trust.

RETIREMENT ACCOUNTS. Most employment retirement plans, as well as IRAs, Keoghs, and other pension plans, have beneficiary designations. They operate in essentially the same manner as the other accounts listed above. The administrator of the plan can give you the appropriate beneficiary designation documents.

**The Important Legal Concept to Remember: If your desire is to get what you own to the person you love quickly and cheaply, pay-on-death accounts are a good way to go.**

# 27

# LIFE INSURANCE

*The importance of life insurance*
*Types of life insurance*
*Two ways to avoid all taxes on life insurance benefits*
*A plan of action*

THE IMPORTANCE OF LIFE INSURANCE. Life insurance is almost always *critical* to the estate-planning process. This must be underscored. The only time life insurance is not needed is if you were to die today and you would have enough money to protect everyone you want to protect, in a manner you would be happy with, and could also afford to pay all possible death taxes. Otherwise, if you are planning your estate, you need life insurance, period. While the amount and type will vary, depending upon your circumstances, the need and requirement for life insurance is usually fundamental to proper estate planning.

There are many reasons to have life insurance, and whether your estate is worth $60,000 or $600,000, one surely applies to you.

1. *To protect your young children:* If you are relatively young, say, in your thirties or forties, then you are likely still in the asset-accumulation stage of financial planning. You are still earning a living, paying off a mortgage, building a nest egg.

If you live long enough, you can create an estate to give to your mate and children. If you do not, and you are the primary wage earner, then there will be no estate to pass on to your family when you die *unless* you buy life insurance. Life insurance not only insures your life, then, but also ensures that of your family. And, for the cost (see below), it simply cannot be beat.

2. *To protect an estate:* If you are in your fifties or sixties, then you likely have a hard-earned, much-deserved estate. Life insurance is equally critical. If your estate will go through probate (because you chose a will), if estate taxes will be due (because the value of your estate is more than $600,000), or if you don't want your heirs to have to sell your property to pay your debts, then life insurance is needed.

3. *To create quick cash:* After a death, there is usually a need for ready cash to pay lawyers, probate fees, funeral expenses, estate taxes, bills, mortgages, etc. Because life insurance is payable almost immediately upon the death of the insured, proceeds can be used to pay for these things. If you use life insurance in conjunction with a trust, then you have the added benefit of being able to name a trustee to oversee the use of these funds.

4. *To avoid probate:* Life insurance is another of many probate-avoidance techniques, and one of the best. The proceeds are payable directly to the beneficiary and thereby completely avoid probate. Note that although the benefits bypass probate, the total amount paid is considered part of your taxable estate, and thereby subject to federal estate taxes by your estate. With proper planning, though, these taxes can be completely avoided.

TYPES OF LIFE INSURANCE.\ There are basically two types of life insurance—term and cash-value (sometimes called whole life) life insurance. These two types of life insurance are analogous to real estate: term life insurance is like renting, and cash-value life insurance is like owning. Note, however, that while whole life may sound attractive at first blush, there are some major drawbacks to owning this type of life insurance (discussed below.)

Like renting, term life insurance is cheaper than cash-value life. And just as you would build up no equity in a home you rented, so too do you build up no equity in the term policy. You "rent" the policy for a specific term, and if you die within that term, the policy pays off. Like a lease, if you do not renew the policy, your rights to collect under it expire once the term ends. Because the policy pays only for the term, and because you build up no ownership interest or equity in the policy, term life is far cheaper than cash-value life. At the end of the term, the policy can be renewed, but usually only after the owner passes a new physical examination.

By way of example, a term policy of $500,000 for a man thirty-five years old may cost about $50 a month. The owner could pay that premium for ten years (total cost: $6,000), and if he died within that ten years, his beneficiaries would get $500,000. If that sounds like gambling, that's because it is. The insurance company is betting that you will outlive the policy, and that it will get to pocket the $6,000 without paying a dime. The morose irony of life insurance is that if you die, you win.

Cash-value life, on the other hand, is like owning real estate. The policy costs more, but it builds up equity as the years and payments progress. Whole life is the type of insurance most often thought of when people think of cash-value life. Unlike term life, which is renewable at the option of the insurance company, whole life, with its ownership characteristics, is usually renewable at the option of the owner of the policy without a new physical exam.

The problem with whole life is that it is really quite expensive, and the returns are not usually worth the investment. Furthermore, it takes quite a while to build up enough equity in the policy to make it even remotely attractive. As a rule of thumb, term life insurance is usually the better way to go.

One final type of insurance that may be of interest to a well-off would-be estate planner is **joint life insurance**. The advantage of this kind of policy is that while it insures two people, usually spouses, it pays only after the second death. At first blush this may seem rather odd, but not so upon closer inspection. Remember that it is fairly simple to pass at least $600,000 tax-free to a spouse or child at the death of the first spouse. It is after the death of the second spouse where taxes come due, absent extensive estate plans. If there is no life insurance to pay these often substantial federal estate taxes, children are often forced to liquidate large chunks of the estate to pay the taxes. Many times, these sales are done at "fire sale" prices since federal estate taxes are due a mere nine months after a death. If the real estate or stock market is down, children may be forced to sell a good portion of their inheritance to pay death taxes.

Joint life insurance prevents this. Either in a living trust, in an irrevocable life insurance trust, or by leaving proper instructions in a will, the proceeds from a joint life insurance policy can be earmarked to pay taxes and protect the estate.

TWO WAYS TO AVOID ALL TAXES ON LIFE INSURANCE BENE-FITS. Sometimes, but not always, life insurance comes tax-free. Taxes apply only if your taxable estate, including the benefits paid, will exceed $600,000. Although the proceeds to a policy *owned by you* are not taxed as income to the recipient, the gross proceeds paid count toward the size of your taxable estate. Similarly, even if the proceeds do not put you over the top, it might create an estate for your spouse in excess of $600,000. In either case, federal estate taxes will be due on the excess.

Mitch and Ali had a combined estate worth $300,000. Before he died, Mitch bought an insurance policy with a face value of $400,000, payable to Ali. When he did die, Mitch's estate was worth $550,000 ($400,000 plus his half of the estate—$150,000). No estate taxes were due. However, when Ali dies, her estate will be worth $700,000, $100,000 of which will be taxed at 37 percent—$37,000.

That $37,000 is a lot of money to give to Uncle Sam, especially when it can be avoided. There are two ways to do so:

· *Give ownership of the policy away*: Like the rest of your estate, only that which you own at the time of your death is considered part of your taxable estate. But if you do not own a life insurance policy, then the proceeds are not part of your estate, and taxes are thereby eluded. The trick, therefore, is to have someone besides you own the policy. If the insured does not own the policy at his death, then the proceeds are not considered part of his taxable estate and no tax is due. This transfer can be done fairly easily.

1. Anyone can transfer (assign) her life insurance policy to anyone else. The first thing to do is to have your life insurance agent prepare a transfer of the policy to someone you trust and notify the insurance company of the change. Although you lose control of the policy (e.g., you can't change the beneficiary if you don't own the policy), you gain the ability to transfer large sums of money tax-free to your loved ones upon your death. Also, you cannot maintain "incidents of ownership" over the policy. That is, you cannot do a sham transfer, remain in control of the policy, and expect the IRS to believe that this was a legitimate transfer, because it will not.

2. Transfer the policy at least three years before you die. Although this is obviously impossible to plan, it is nonetheless important to know. If you die within three years of the transfer, the transfer is disallowed by the IRS.

3. After the transfer, the new owner must make all premium payments. It is possible for the old owner to give the new owner the money for the premium payments, and if

the amount is less than $10,000 a year, no one will be any the wiser.

· *Create an ILIT*: Using an irrevocable life insurance trust is similar to the method above, with the real difference being that it is a trust, and not a relative, who will own the policy. *You cannot be the trustee*, since that would be an "incident of ownership." By naming someone else as the trustee, and by transferring funds sufficient to pay the premiums into the trust yearly, you get the policy out of your estate.

When you do die, the proceeds go to the ILIT and can then be used by your spouse. When she dies, the proceeds will not be part of her estate either, and the remains of the fund can go to your children tax-free. The downside to an ILIT is that it is irrevocable; the trust cannot later be changed without court approval.

A PLAN OF ACTION. Term life insurance is the most cost-effective way to secure your family's future. *Buy as much as you can afford*. If you can afford whole life, buy that. This is some of the best advice you can follow.

**The Important Legal Concept to Remember: Life insurance is one of the easiest, least expensive estate-planning options available. Buy as much as you can afford.**

# 28

# PLANNING FOR A DISABILITY

Living wills

Durable health-care power of attorney

What to do with completed forms

Aside from deciding how to transfer their assets after death, older people have the added concern of the possible deterioration of their health. Should that happen, decisions, both financial and health, must be made. While a properly designed living trust can deal with financial concerns, there are also two ways to assure that proper health-care decisions are made.

LIVING WILLS. Although a living will sounds like a living trust, they have nothing at all in common. A living will is a document sometimes called a "directive to physician." It tells your physician what kind of health care you wish to have done, or not done, should you become terminally ill or incapacitated. Your physician must follow your directions or transfer you to a doctor who will. In it, you can state

· That no extraordinary measures should be taken on your behalf. Extraordinary measures includes things like administration of food and water to keep you alive, the use of ventilators to keep you breathing, or the use of medication to ease pain. Maybe you may want pain relief but nothing else. It is up to you.

· That all extraordinary measures must be taken to revive you and keep you alive.

Many health-care providers have preprinted living will forms. All you need to do is sign the document and (usually) have it witnessed.

DURABLE HEALTH-CARE POWER OF ATTORNEY. Like a durable special power of attorney for financial decisions, a health-care power of attorney (sometimes called a medical proxy) permits you to name someone to make health-care decisions on your behalf when you are no longer able to do so for yourself. In it, you appoint someone (your "attorney-in-fact") who understands what you want done to deal with your doctors and make your decisions. Similar to a living will, a health-care power of attorney can specify what sorts of measures you want taken.

Your attorney-in-fact should certainly be someone whose judgment you value. He or she should also be someone who can be around in case you become disabled and will be in the hospital for an extended period of time. A sister in a distant city may seem like the right person, but if she cannot be at the hospital every day, appointing her would be pointless. It is also smart to pick an alternate should your choice be unable to serve.

As with a living will, most health-care providers have preprinted health-care power-of-attorney forms. A good course of action is to have both a living will and a health-care power of attorney so that your wishes will be clear and will be followed.

WHAT TO DO WITH COMPLETED FORMS. It is a good idea to have your documents signed and witnessed in front of a notary public. The fee is minimal. After the documents have been signed, witnessed, and notarized, have copies made and sent to your doctor, your attorney-in-fact, your health-care provider, your lawyer, and a relative or close friend.

**The Important Legal Concept to Remember: You have a constitutional right to make your own decisions about your body. Despite a life-threatening illness, you can make sure that your desires are followed by obtaining and signing the right documents.**

# APPENDICES

# COMMON QUESTIONS
# AND ANSWERS

## THE NEED FOR AN ESTATE PLAN

*I cannot really afford a lawyer, so what do I do?*
If you cannot afford an attorney, then you probably do not have enough assets to warrant a living trust. A will should do fine, and the one in this book can be used as a prototype. You should also check out Section V, "Other Estate-planning Options," to get an idea of some other methods of estate planning you can utilize that do not require legal assistance.

## PREPARATION

*Can't I give my half of my joint tenancy property away in my will?*
No. You do not own a divisible half of any joint tenancy property. If you own it with your wife, however, you can both transfer it to a joint living trust.

*Is probate really so bad?*
Yes.

*Is a living trust the only way to avoid probate?*
No. Other methods include giving your property away before you die, owning property in joint tenancy (only sometimes a

good idea), and naming a beneficiary on accounts such as life insurance, retirement plans, and pay-on-death accounts.

*My estate is only worth about $50,000. Will it go through probate? Will my estate have to pay death taxes?*
It is unlikely that your estate will go through probate since every state has a small-estate exception to the probate laws. It depends upon the laws of your state. Check with an attorney. Estate taxes are due only on estates over $600,000.

## WILLS

*What if I die without a will?*
Each state's probate proceedings are designed to distribute your property to your nearest relatives. If you have no living relatives, your state will likely end up owning your property.

*I heard that I can write my will in my own hand. True?*
A will written in your own hand is called a holographic will. About half of all states accept holographic wills, although the exact requirements vary from state to state. As a *general* rule, the entire will must be written in your own handwriting. *Do not type it.* It must be dated and signed by you, and witnesses are usually not required.

*When do I need to change my will?*
If you get divorced. If one of your beneficiaries dies. If you want to change or add a beneficiary. If you inherit a lot of money. If you move from or to a community property state.

*What should I do with my will after it is completed?*
Your will needs to be stored in a safe place, preferably at home. Safe deposit boxes at banks are sealed upon your death and may be difficult to get into. Your will should also be copied, and copies should be kept with your attorney and/or executor. It is the *original will* that is *required* by the probate court, so make sure that your executor and attorney know where the original is.

## LIVING TRUSTS

*I am worried that if I make a living trust, I will lose control of my property. Is that right?*
It is absolutely wrong. Because you make the trust, you are the trustee during your life, and you are the beneficiary during your life, you will see no changes at all after your living trust is done. If you are unhappy with your trust, simply revoke it.

*I have adult children. Do I need a children's subtrust?*
Not really. Children's subtrusts are usually used to care for minor children. However, if you will be leaving substantial sums of money to an adult child, you might consider it. Inheriting a lot of money is not always an easy thing. It can induce laziness or indulgence. Spreading the money out at different times may help to avoid this.

*I have heard of will contests, but not trust contests. Is there such a thing?*
A trust can be contested, but it is more difficult. Unhappiness with a will is not a legally justifiable reason to contest it. A properly drafted trust is evidence in and of itself that the maker was competent, so trust contests are difficult and rare.

*My wife and I both have lots of separate property, aside from our joint property. Should we still have a joint trust?*
There is no reason not to. Your living trust can easily designate where each of you wants your separate property to go.

*What happens to my creditors' claims against my estate if I have a living trust?*
Use of a will guarantees probate, and probate gives your creditors a chance to get paid. With a living trust probate is avoided, but your estate still may owe money to creditors. The difference is that it will be far more difficult for your creditors to find your assets and beneficiaries with a living trust. Nevertheless, the law is that your beneficiaries are liable for your debts, up to the amount they inherit. Creditors usually have twelve months to make a claim against the trust.

*What assurances do I have that my trustee will follow my instructions?*

Your trustee is a fiduciary, which is the highest responsibility imposed by law. If your trustee breaches his fiduciary duty, he could be found *personally liable*, and could *lose personal assets* as a result. Also, if he does not follow your instructions, your beneficiaries can go to court and have him removed. If this is a legitimate concern, either rethink your choice of trustee, pick cotrustees, or choose an institution as trustee.

## OTHER ESTATE-PLANNING OPTIONS

*Can I give a gift to someone that is worth more than $10,000?*

Sure. The $10,000 "limit" is only with regard to gift taxes. Gifts under that amount pay no gift tax; gifts over pay the tax.

*We own our house as joint tenants. Should we change that designation?*

Probably. A married couple without many other assets can keep a house as joint tenants and thereby avoid probate. If you want to you could change it to a tenancy in common. This will enable each of you to give away your half. If you plan to have a living trust, the trust should own the house. It really depends on how many other assets you own and how old you are.

*What is the difference between a living trust and a living will?*

A living trust relates to your financial decisions. A living will deals with your health-care decisions.

# GLOSSARY

**A-B Trust**: Also known as a bypass trust and a marital support trust. This type of trust allows the beneficiary to use trust assets during his life but retains the principal for a different, final beneficiary.

**Affidavit**: A voluntary statement of facts made under oath.

**Alternate Beneficiary**: The person who will receive a gift in a will or living trust if the primary beneficiary passes away before the testator or trust maker.

**Alternate Residuary Beneficiary**: The person who will receive the residuary estate should the residuary beneficiary die before the testator or trust maker.

**Assign**: To transfer any type of property or right to another.

**Bar Association**: An association of lawyers found on local, state, and national levels.

**Beneficiary**: Someone who benefits from an act of another. As used in estate planning, someone who is to receive a gift from the testator or trust maker.

**Bequest**: A gift of personal property in a will.

**Bypass Trust**: Also known as an A-B trust and a marital support trust. This type of trust allows the beneficiary to use trust assets during his life but retains the principal for a different, final beneficiary.

**Capital Gains Tax**: A provision in the income tax laws providing that profits from the sale of a capital asset are taxed at a certain rate. Profits from the sale of homes and stocks often result in the need to pay a capital gains tax.

**Charitable Lead Trust**: An irrevocable trust made for a charity that permits the charity to receive the income from the property for a set number of years. When the period is over, the asset reverts back to the trust maker's estate.

**Charitable Remainder Trust**: An irrevocable trust made in favor of a charity that allows the trust maker to keep the income generated by assets in the trust for use during his lifetime.

**Codicil**: A supplement or addition to an existing will that may modify, add to, subtract from, or otherwise change the will.

**Common Law States**: The forty-one states that, among other things, look to title to determine property ownership.

**Community Property States**: The nine states that look to acquisition during marriage to determine property ownership.

**Conditional Bequest**: A gift that is made only after certain conditions are first met.

**Cotrustee**: One of two or more trustees of a trust.

**Death Taxes**: Also known as federal estate taxes, they are levied upon the property of a person who died when the taxable value of that property exceeds $600,000.

**Decedent**: A deceased person.

**Deed**: A writing signed by the owner of real estate that transfers title to the property to another.

**Devise**: A gift of real estate made in a will.

**Disinherit**: The act by which the owner of an estate deprives someone of an inheritance.

**Domicile**: That place where a person has his residence.

**Donor**: Someone who gives a gift.

**Durable Health-Care Power of Attorney**: A document that

authorizes a named person to act and make health-care decisions on behalf of another.

**Durable Special Power of Attorney**: A document that authorizes a named person to act and make legal decisions on behalf of another.

**Estate**: The total property of whatever kind owned by a decedent at the time of his death.

**Estate Plan**: A plan whereby estate assets are preserved, taxes and probate fees reduced, and family cared for. It may be as simple as a will or as complicated as a living trust with additions.

**Execution**: As it pertains to a will, performing all acts necessary to effectuate the will, including the signing and witnessing of it.

**Executor/Executrix**: The person appointed by the testator to carry out the directions and requests in the will.

**Family Pot Trust**: A type of children's trust that keeps all money in one "pot" to use as necessary by the trustee for all beneficiaries.

**Fiduciary**: A person who has a duty to act primarily for another's benefit. A fiduciary must act with scrupulous good faith and candor.

**Generation-skipping Trust**: A tax-savings trust in which one's children have access to trust income, but the trust principal is left for one's grandchildren.

**Gift**: A voluntary transfer of property to another made gratuitously.

**Guardian**: A person lawfully invested with the power and charged with the duty of taking care of the child of the testator while the child is a minor.

**Heir**: A person who is entitled by law to inherit an estate if the testator left no will or living trust. Usually spouses, children, and parents are heirs of a decedent, in that order.

**Holographic Will**: A will that is entirely written, dated, and signed by the hand of the testator herself.

**ILIT**: An irrevocable life insurance trust designed to own a life insurance policy in order to keep it out of the taxable estate of the trust maker.

**Inherit**: To receive property from someone who has died.

**Interested Person**: A person who has a legal interest in the estate of the deceased. Generally, applies only to heirs or people named in a previous will.

**Intestate**: A person is said to die intestate when he dies without making a will or other valid estate-transfer document.

**Irrevocable**: That which cannot be revoked or recalled.

**Joint Life Insurance**: Life insurance on two people, usually spouses, that is payable upon the death of the second person.

**Joint Marital Assets**: Marital assets owned jointly by both husband and wife.

**Joint Tenancy**: A form of ownership on real or personal property whose main characteristic is that, upon the death of the first joint tenant, the property transfers by law to the other joint tenant outside of probate.

**Life Insurance**: A contract between the holder of the policy and the insurance company whereby the company agrees to pay a specified sum to the owner's designated beneficiary upon the death of the insured in exchange for payment of premiums.

**Living Trust**: A trust created while a person is alive that stays in effect until her death. Also called an intervivos trust.

**Living Will**: A document that indicates what type of life-sustaining measures someone wants taken on his behalf.

**Marital Support Trust**: Also known as a bypass trust and an A-B trust. This type of trust allows the beneficiary to use trust assets during his life but retains the principal for a different, final beneficiary.

**Marital Trust**: A subtrust of a living trust made for the benefit of a surviving spouse that is designed to protect privacy and shield trust assets from creditors.

**Minor:** A person under eighteen years of age.

**Net Value:** The remainder when liabilities are deducted from assets.

**No-Contest Clause:** A provision in a will that states that a gift is given upon the condition that the beneficiary does not contest the will.

**Pay-on-Death Account:** A type of financial account that designates a beneficiary to inherit the remains of the account when the owner of the account dies.

**Personal Property:** All property other than real estate. It usually connotes money and goods.

**Personal Representative:** Sometimes known as the executor or administrator of an estate in probate, this is the person authorized to see the case through probate.

**Pour-Over Will:** A will that transfers property into a trust.

**Pretermitted Heir Statute:** A statute that provides for a child or other descendent of the testator, unintentionally omitted in the will, to nevertheless receive a portion of the decedent's estate.

**Primary Beneficiary:** A person who is to receive a specific gift in a will.

**Principal:** The property put into a trust. Trust principal could be property or money.

**Probate:** The court procedure by which a will is proved to be valid or invalid, which appoints executors or administrators, identifies heirs, pays debts, and distributes property to heirs or beneficiaries.

**Prudent Investor Rule:** A legal axiom that requires that a trustee must invest trust funds prudently.

**QTIP Trust:** A marital tax-savings trust in which property is left for a spouse for use during his life. No taxes are assessed on the property until the death of the second spouse.

**Real Estate:** Land, and whatever is erected upon, growing on, or affixed to that land.

**Residuary Beneficiary**: That person who is to receive all property left in an estate not otherwise specifically given away.

**Revoke**: To cancel, annul, rescind, repeal, or make void by taking back.

**Sole Ownership**: That property owned by someone to which no one else has any claim or right. Separate property.

**Special Needs Trust**: A kind of trust that is designed and intended to care for a special needs child. Government assistance eligibility can be preserved, and a willing trustee can be named to help the child.

**Spendthrift Trust**: A trust created to care for a beneficiary, but which secures trust assets from improvidence or incapacity.

**Subtrust**: A trust that is made part of a living trust which is designed to care for someone other than the original trust maker and which will last beyond the living trust.

**Successor Trustee**: The person designated in the trust to be the trustee in case the trust maker becomes incapacitated, or who will be the trustee of an ongoing subtrust.

**Taxable Estate**: The portion of the estate that is subject to federal estate taxes. Usually calculated by subtracting liabilities from assets.

**Tenancy by the Entirety**: A tenancy between spouses with a right of survivorship.

**Tenancy in Common**: A form of tenancy whereby each owner holds a proportional interest in the property.

**Testamentary Capacity**: The mental ability recognized by law as sufficient for making a will. Generally includes an understanding of the contents of one's estate and will.

**Testamentary Trust**: A trust that is made as part of a will and comes into effect only after the testator dies.

**Testator**: The will maker.

**Title**: Ownership of property. Usually associated with real estate.

**Totten Trust**: Also known as a pay-on-death bank account. A bank account that designates a beneficiary to inherit the remains of the account when the owner of the account dies.

**Trustee**: The person or institution who manages the trust for the benefit of the beneficiaries.

**Trust Maker**: Also known as the grantor, settlor, or trustor. A person who makes a trust.

**Waive/Waiver**: The voluntary relinquishment of a known right.

**Will**: A document by which a person disposes of his property that takes effect after his death.

**Will Contest**: A controversy concerning the eligibility of an instrument in probate.

**Will Substitute**: Any number of devises used instead of a will to dispose of property. Common will substitutes include living trusts and joint tenancy.

# TWO TYPICAL
# ESTATE PLANS

Phil and Mindy are in their thirties and have three minor children. They own their own home as joint tenants. Phil works full-time, Mindy part-time. Aside from their house, they own two cars, some personal belongings, and a modest savings account. In all, the gross value of their estate is around $100,000. Their main goal with their estate plan is to make sure there is enough money for the kids to get through college.

Since they do not own many assets, cannot afford an expensive living trust, and are unlikely to die soon, Phil and Mindy decide to have separate wills drawn up. They name each other as the primary beneficiary of their estates.

They also each create a testamentary children's trust as part of their wills, and name the trust as the alternate beneficiary of the estate. If Mindy dies first, Phil will be the trustee, and Phil's sister Robyn will be the alternate trustee. If Phil dies first, Mindy will be the trustee, and Phil's sister Robyn will be the alternate trustee. They also name Robyn and her husband to be the personal guardians of the children should Phil and Mindy die together.

In order to secure the financial future of their children, each takes out a $100,000 term life insurance policy. Each names the children's trust as the beneficiary. Their instructions in the testamentary children's trust state that the money should be used to care for the health, education, and welfare of all three kids based upon need. Whatever money remains will be divided equally when the youngest child reaches the age of twenty-five.

Phil and Mindy also have durable health-care powers of attorney and living wills drawn up for each of them.

By naming each other as the primary beneficiary, each spouse will inherit the entire estate. Because the house is held in joint tenancy, it does not need to go through probate. While either spouse is alive, he or she will be the trustee of the children's trust. When the second spouse dies, another $100,000 will go into the trust, and Robyn will be the trustee. Richard is a wealthy widower in his sixties. He has two adult children and three grandchildren. He owns two homes, a few cars, and many financial investments. His entire estate is worth $1 million. His main estate-planning goal is to preserve as much of his estate as possible for his loved ones.

Richard decides that a living trust and a subtrust will accomplish his goals. He transfers all of his assets into the trust, and also has a pour-over will drawn up so that any later-bought assets will also go into the trust.

His living trust states that upon his death his successor trustee should give $300,000 outright to each of his two adult children, thereby using his $600,000 exemption. He takes the last $400,000 and puts it into a generation-skipping trust for his grandchildren. While his two children are alive, they will use the proceeds of the generation-skipping trust. When they die, the grandchildren will get the principal outright.

Richard also has a durable health-care power of attorney and a living will drawn up.

Richard's living trust avoids probate and its attendant fees. The GST avoids federal estate taxes. Richard's plan will successfully transfer $1 million probate- and tax-free.

# INDEX